ACTING GOOD OR BAD?
Break into film and TV: avoid making mistakes and create success

F.G. FRASER

Acting Good or Bad?

First Edition Published by Francesca Fraser

Copyright © 2024 by Francesca Fraser

ISBN: 9798340466761

All rights reserved. Neither this book, nor any parts within it may be sold or reproduced in any form without permission.

No part of this book may be reproduced in any form or by any electronic or mechanical means including information storage and retrieval systems, without permission in writing from the author. The only exception is by a reviewer, who may quote short excerpts in a review.

The purpose of this book is to educate and entertain. The views and opinions expressed in this book are that of the author based on her personal experiences and education. The author does not guarantee that anyone following the techniques, suggestions, ideas or strategies will become successful.

The author shall neither be liable nor responsible for any loss or damage allegedly arising from any information or suggestion in this book.

Dedication

Driven by my hunger and determination to succeed in the world of film and television, I found myself on the sets of various productions, including some of the most prestigious A-list Hollywood films. My journey was far from smooth, filled with challenges and learning experiences.

Through this book, I aim to share the lessons I've learned, helping you avoid the mistakes I made and providing you with the knowledge you need to thrive in this industry. I learned by observing and adapting, and now, I've compiled all that wisdom here for you.

Good luck, and may you achieve all your dreams and turn them into reality.

Table of Contents

Foreword 6
About the Author 8
To My Wonderful Reader, ... 10
Testimonials 11

Learn SOME OF the Lingo 13
Chapter 1: Do you really want to be an actor? 18
Chapter 2: Self-Knowing 23
Chapter 3: Mistakes to Avoid: Part 1 30
Chapter 4: Theatre acting vs film and TV 42
Chapter 5: Headshots 45
Chapter 6: Showreels 61
Chapter 7: Casting Websites 63
Chapter 8: Castings/Auditions 76
Chapter 9: Spotlight 82
Chapter 10: Getting an Agent 84
Chapter 11: Let go of Desperation 88

Chapter 12: Mistakes to Avoid: Part 2 98

Chapter 13: Mistakes to Avoid: Part 3 111

Chapter 14: Mistakes to Avoid: Part 4 116

Chapter 15: Mistakes to Avoid: Part 5 121

Chapter 16: Dissipate the ego 128

Thank You 141

Foreword

This book contains a lot of vital knowledge and tools needed for anyone to start their acting journey.

I taught Francesca, some of the tools in this book, that I learnt while studying to become a film director at RADA (Royal Academy of Dramatic Art, the number one drama school in the country!)

This book is a simple guide to help anyone get started in the film and TV industry. I highly recommend reading all of her books!

Francesca shares some of her personal stories that are entertaining and thrilling. She is open and honest about the mistakes that she made, so you can avoid making the same mistakes.

Foreword

Francesca also shares the secrets that helped her succeed in her auditions.

Richard Standeven, award-winning film director. Many of his impressive Film and TV credits include, "Band of Gold." "Falling for a Dancer." "Cracker." "Between the lines." "Ballykiss Angel" and most recently "Waking the Dead."

*Richard has always been a good friend and has never hurt me. He is not the film director I have mentioned in this book or my other book.

About the Author

Francesca was born in Brighton on August 14, 1986, making her 38 years old in 2024. She is passionate about staying fit and healthy, both mentally and physically. Her fitness routine includes boxing classes, swimming, nature walks, running 5km three times a week, and lifting weights.

Francesca thrives on being in front of the camera, performing alongside other actors. She also enjoys the camaraderie of being on set, whether in the foreground or background, meeting like-minded actors in films and music videos.

Her career has brought her into close contact with some of the biggest names in the film and music industry. She once held hands with a Hollywood star, shared a smile and eye contact with another, and stood so close to a third that they almost touched. On another occasion, a world-famous musician struck up a conversation with her about the

About the Author

paintings on the wall, a topic she had just been discussing with someone else. Had he been watching her?

Francesca's life on and off set has been filled with incredible experiences. She is eager to share her journey and tips to help you reach your dreams.

To My Wonderful Reader,

Thank you for being a beacon of light in a world that can sometimes feel dark and harsh. I hope your journey has been kind to you, even though many of us face significant challenges along the way.

I'm thrilled that you've chosen to read my book. Within these pages, you'll find simple yet vital tips that can guide you toward success more swiftly than my path. The insights I share come from my personal experiences and lessons learned. While not every piece of advice may be perfect, most of it is exactly what you need to know.

Thank you for taking the time to read my book. Remember to let your inner star shine brightly for the world to see.

Warm regards,
F. G. Fraser

Testimonials

"Frankie is a beautiful soul. She is always willing to help me with anything when I ask and has even done some fashion and beauty modelling for my book series "Model Diaries"!"

—Deborah Jay Kelly, Celebrity Red Carpet host, the owner and CEO of The Angel Academy of Teaching and Training, Model, and Author.

"Frankie told me the steps to get modelling jobs, and I have had a lot of fun in achieving success. I only ever take on paid work now."

—Carlos M Fandango

"Frankie has a lot of compassion for all beings. When I was struggling, she was there for me and helped guide me. For that I will always be grateful".

—Stuart Waite, Service Advisor from Sittingbourne.

F.G. Fraser

"Frankie is a very charismatic person and wise too. She knows what she is talking about and has a huge heart wanting to help all kinds of people. She helped me out of a very dark place. Read her books and you will one hundred percent discover something that will help you."

—**Omoyemi Fatusin,**
IT professional, Milton Keynes.

"Francesca is a wise and effective communicator. At a point in my darkness, she helped me embrace the feeling and be comfortable enough to do nothing but wait . . . wait and listen. This virtual request saved me from an impulsive decision, and I will forever be grateful for her wisdom and love."

—**Keneilwe,**
Digital project manager, Cape Town.

Learn SOME OF the Lingo

When you start getting roles, even if it is a background role you may start hearing words and phrases you haven't come across before; so, I have written you a list here to begin with.

Off book – all your lines from the script are learnt off by heart.

Location – the place where you first meet up, which is also usually called "crowd base" if you're a SA. Sometimes you get taken by minibus to a separate "crowd base" location.

Call time – The time you are given to arrive at the specific location given to you if you are confirmed for your role in the film shoot.

Shoot – This is the day and the place where the filming takes place. The whole day of the filming event, for the scene or scenes.

Pencilled – Before being confirmed for a film shoot you will be pencilled in for the date of the shoot. This isn't a definite confirmation of work, but some agencies tell you to keep yourself free for the date, regardless of if they decide to choose you or not. One of the frustrating parts of being a Supporting artist.

Costume fitting – this one is easily translated.

But YES, normal clothes and outfits that even a passerby in the background wears, is a costume! Fascinating! I always imagined a costume to be the outfit stage actors wear, but nope, it also applies in TV and film! Sometimes you will be asked to supply your own and other times you will be invited to a location and also receive payment for it.

Wardrobe – The place where the costumes are held and where the costume fitter's fit you for your costume.

Headshot – This is a professional photograph of the head and shoulders, something an actor must have to show to casting directors.

Showreel – This is a short video clip of an actor showing off their talent to send to casting directors in hope to secure an audition for a role.

Supporting artist (or S.A.) – Not the lead actor or other acting roles with fewer lines. Also, called a background artist.

Learn SOME OF the Lingo

Featured role – When a supporting artist gets a role that is visible on screen.

Crowd Base (sometimes called a green room) – The place where SAs and sometimes actors will be held before and after being called onto the set. This is also the place where you will put your costume on and get your hair and make-up done. Many times, you will get your hair and make-up done, put your costume on, and then be transported to the crowd base at a separate location.

Director – The person in charge of the whole scene and the whole movie. They direct the actors and the props and the positioning of the cameras.

Casting Director – Chooses the selection of actors or actresses for the Director to choose from. The casting director also chooses all the supporting artists for the background.

AD – An assistant director. As a SA, you will have an assistant director telling you what to do and where to stand or sit. Depending on how many SA's there are, there maybe more than one AD. They take orders through an earpiece from the director.

The set/ onset – This is the most terrifying, but also the most exciting place to be. This is where the filming takes place and the main actors and cameras are. An AD will collect you from the crowd base and take you there, then the AD will position you and explain the scene.

Stand-in – He or she stands or sits in the same spot as the main actor while the camera crew sets up the cameras and puts them into focus, etc.

Take/ between takes – A take is when the camera is rolling, and the actors are performing their scene. Everyone behind the camera must be silent and focused, and all artists must be performing their designated action until the director calls out "cut" which means you can stop and relax.

Re-set – When the director calls out "re-set" after "cut", it means everyone must get back to their first positions at the beginning of the scene, so another take can be made.

Rolling – When you hear this being called out it is an extremely important cue that everyone on set must be silent as filming a take is about to begin. It means the camera is on and filming and the sound is rolling and recording. A lot of the time you will hear, "camera set, sound set".

Action – If you enjoy behind-the-scenes documentaries about filmmaking, you will be familiar with this one. When the director says "action" a short time after "rolling" it means that the actors start performing their actions and lines for the scene.

If there are background artists included in the scene then "background action" will be called before "action".

Wrap – "That's a wrap" is called out to signal that the filming for that day has come to an end and everyone can go home.

Learn SOME OF the Lingo

After a long day's work, everyone, including the SAs who weren't used in the scene filmed on that day are extremely pleased. Sometimes, if it was a short day, or the cast thought it would be a longer day and thought they would be filming some more after a break, they can be made to feel a bit disappointed.

Boom – This is the word for the microphone.

Hero shot – If you have an acting role and the director calls out, "hero shot", this means you need to be slightly bigger with the movement. Imagine a change of emotion while holding something, the thing you're holding must also be in shot. The audience must see what you're holding or seeing that makes you (your character) feel a certain way.

Insert acting – This is the acting between dialogue, but it can also be a long piece of acting that has a lot of changes in emotions.

For example, imagine a horror movie where the victim is running away from the killer, and then the victim just about reaches safety by seeing an escape route, then suddenly out of nowhere, the killer pounces on the victim. The victim then realises they used to be best friends with the killer and attempts to change the killer's mind by getting to their emotions with a memory. Perhaps showing them a best friend necklace or bracelet, they wear.

A lot of acting can be done in this scenario without any dialogue.

Chapter 1
Do you really want to be an actor?

First, you need to ask yourself, "Is this something I really want to do?" and then you need to ask yourself, "Why is it something I want to do?

If your heart isn't really in it, then it is not something you should do, and here's why. If it is for "fame and fortune" then that is not a reason to go into it.

When I was a small child and I first learned that fame and fortune could be a part of it, my inner thought was, "I am going to show everyone and anyone that has ever hurt me or done wrong by me. I will show them all!" It came from pain and wanting to get back at people. Show them who they messed with, is a true superstar! My reason now is more to show you, that if I can do it, then so can you.

Do you really want to be an actor?

(I was recently thinking about a person in my life being unkind to me, and I felt another huge angry push to succeed properly in my chosen career. So, perhaps it is not such a bad reason after all?)

This book is a step of mine to get me to go further in my chosen career, I believe that if we choose to be loving and help others, we will always succeed.

If you don't feel loved and you feel bitter resentment towards the world, when you do work on growing yourself and eradicating the "ego," which I will discuss later, you may find that perhaps acting is not the career path you wish to follow after all.

When I studied acting for film at film school, one of the key things we were taught was to let go of our ego. The ego is not part of being able to get into character and be present because to get into character you must lose all of yourself, the identity your ego sees as being you.

If acting is something your heart truly desires because you love watching movies, you love seeing how they're created and you want to give audiences a thrilling experience, then this is the exact reason you should go into it. Also, it is an escape from reality and a vessel to express yourself.

When creating movies, whether you're writing, directing, or acting, your involvement is so immersed that you are getting a thrilling experience while doing it, thinking about the finished result. However, an inexperienced onlooker may think it is stressful and pressurized. The feeling of knowing you nailed your role in the film or TV production is extremely satisfying. It can be stressful, like any job, but the result is worth the pain.

The film director on set and all the crew members around, just want to nail their job and get the job done to what is seen as perfection, and as an actor or actress, you need to feel ok with this.

When you are on set, you may have to repeat the same scene, the same dialogue, and the same actions again and again. If you get bored or frustrated doing the same thing repeatedly, it is not the industry you should get into. A lot of the time it just needs to be filmed from a different angle, and not because any mistakes were made.

If your ego will be bruised by being told abruptly and sometimes impolitely what to do, then acting is not for you. As a SA it is even worse as you are seen as the lesser part of the crew and not treated with as much respect as others. This is not fun for the ego at all. If you cannot tolerate being thought of as less than anyone else onset, then being an SA really isn't for you.

Sometimes, you will work with grateful directors who make you feel appreciated, and they seem calm and not stressed out at all.

I have been diagnosed with Asperger syndrome; I refrained from mentioning it in my previous book, "Sex,

Do you really want to be an actor?

Good or Bad?" because I always feel nervous about people's responses to me. I also don't want to be seen as "the person on the autistic spectrum," it is embarrassing. I just want to be seen as a normal human being and be loved and accepted with all my quirks. I certainly don't want to be seen as an outcast which I often found myself as a child and adolescent. I avoided people for a long time even when they tried to interact with me. The risk of being rejected caused too much pain and anxiety.

Part of my condition makes me thrive on routine and predictability. I prefer things to stay consistent. When I first started acting, the constant change of locations was incredibly overwhelming. It took me months to adjust, not only from the stress but also from the excitement of pursuing a career I love. When I am on set and acting out the scene, I have my lines prepared. In some sort of way, I know what to expect. I have been described as "having a dangerous memory," possibly also due to my condition. This description was given by a guy I met and had a romantic interest in, a very long time ago.

I also have my actions prepared if there are any, and acting feels natural now, so it shows through my eyes. The director will have already told me how he would like it done and I will be prepared. It is so much better than normal social interactions where nothing is prepared.

There is a type of acting called improvisation. I never apply for those roles asking for it. It scares the hell out of me. You just spontaneously do and say whatever, of course within the guidelines of what the director wants.

When I have a close relationship with someone and I know they get my humour, I can be rather good at improvisation. It must be a self-confidence and a trust issue. I am learning all the time about myself, on my life journey and I can only practice things and get better.

As I said before, if you want to be an actor for fame and fortune, then it is not the industry you want to be in. Only 1% of all actors are ever working at one time. 99% of actors are out of work or are doing unpaid work. I am not entirely sure of the exact percentages, as my recent acting for film course said 93% of actors are out of work. However, you get the message.

Unpaid work can be good for early experience and for getting show-reel footage, which I will explain more about in another chapter.

Chapter 2
Self-Knowing

Self-belief, or self-knowing, as I prefer to call it, is the most vital step. It is something that I have often deeply struggled with myself, due to various forms of bullying and abuse in my younger life, and with many voices around me saying, "No, you can't do that; you need to get a proper job!". Despite that, miraculously, I still managed to experience success.

Knowing is different from a belief. If you have read or decided to read my other book, "Sex, Good or Bad?" You will see how I know God is real, rather than just merely believing it because I was told to believe it.

(Although I found myself in desperate situations where calling on God was my only source of help, many people are fortunate enough not to face such painful and sometimes dangerous circumstances. I had some belief to call out to God for help in the first place.)

Maybe you're religious? Maybe you're not? Maybe you're an atheist? Or maybe you have your own beliefs? I respect everyone and their beliefs. I reverted to Islam and became Muslim.

When I attempted to pray five times a day, one of my dreams, which I longed for, for years came true. I was part of a huge superstar's music video. When someone believes in God, they continue to believe because they see things that they can only describe as God-giving. An atheist will keep being an atheist because they have not experienced anything that will make them believe.

However, it starts with a belief, then the belief turns into a knowing when evidence shows up after first believing. Think about the many people who are a part of religious communities and have been told about God from a young age. They believe in something that feels good to believe, but how many of these people KNOW? They read and study the designated religious book for the religion they follow. This is all thoughts and choosing to believe what it says. Not one person who reads stories from these books can know that the story happened. They have been taught to believe it is true. They can never actually know. The stories are from thousands of years ago.

Stories that we know are 100% true, are the stories we experience first-hand. Either it happened to us, or we were witnesses to it happening to someone else. When we witness something happening to someone else, we can still make up our version of how we perceive it and interpret it from our point of view, from the experiences we have already experienced in life.

In my first book, I also share more about some of the abuse that I suffered and other events it led to; trauma and abuse that helped me on my acting journey. The other stuff is not so helpful, like getting involved in more abusive situations. I will go into more detail in the "Mistakes to Avoid" chapters.

Back to self-knowing. How can you have self-belief and be self-knowing? Easy, you can read my story about my dad and my auntie.

I am to you, that my dad and my auntie were to me. "If they can do it, then so can I!"

If I can do it, then so can you!

My inspiring Dad and Famous Auntie

When I was merely 6 years old, I was sitting on my dad's lap in front of the television, watching the Australian soap, "Home and Away." I remember getting upset over a car crash scene and the characters being injured. I buried my face into my dad saying, "No, no, no!"

My dad comforted me and explained that the characters on the TV were not real, they were made up. Their real names were different in real life, and they were just acting and playing it out. The blood wasn't real, but only special effects make-up.

I was in total awe and admiration. I started watching the TV through completely different eyes.

I went away and started thinking about what my dad told me. My mind had been completely blown.

Every time I watched a film or a TV program with a child actor, I longed to be the child playing the character. It was almost a feeling of being in agony that it wasn't me.

When sitting on my dad's lap again in front of the television watching actors perform, I told him that I wanted to be on the TV doing what they do.

He then told me and my young impressionable mind, that if that is what I want to do, then that is what I shall do. He said I could do anything I wanted to do if I just put my mind to it. It felt so good. It touched my soul, and I knew it was the truth. I had not been told by anyone that it was hard to get into. I had not heard any negative voices telling me that I couldn't do it either.

My dad once told me that to succeed, I'd need to attend the best acting school in the country: RADA, the Royal Academy of Dramatic Art. Although I haven't made it there yet, I'm determined to enroll in one of their short courses someday. I haven't been to RADA yet, but this August, I'm starting a 4-week "Acting for Film" course at MET Film

Self-Knowing

School in Ealing. At the time of writing, it begins next week, and I'm super excited! I didn't know film school existed until I met someone who went there, and I have since done an "Acting for Film" weekend course at MET film school, located at the oldest film studios in the UK. That is where my auntie would have filmed many of the films she was in, which added excitement to the journey I have been on.

After my dad lifted my spirits and built up my confidence, which he was always good at, he then told me about when he was a young boy and that he played a part in a film called "Dear Octopus" in 1943. He played the character Joe. My father's name was William Alistair Stuart Fraser, but his stage name was Alistair Stewart. He was always called Alistair or Al for short.

My dad then told me how he got the part in the film. I absolutely adored this story, and he wrote about it in his book.

(If you fancy reading about his fascinating life and how he became a self-made millionaire, his book is "The Answer Unleashed" with his author's name being William Fraser.)

My dad told me that his sister Alison, before the Second World War, became a child star. Her stage name was Binkie Stuart. I was thrilled to listen to my Auntie's stories, and I longed to meet her. My dad had a falling out with her before I was born and sadly at that time, I hadn't met her. I always longed to meet her. My famous actress auntie. I felt super excited and knew for a fact that one day, I too could make films and get on set. I thought about her often and beamed for joy, hoping one day my dad would make up with her and I could meet her. Maybe she could even help me get into acting?

One day shortly after World War 2 began, my grandmother was unable to get a babysitter for my father so she could take my auntie to an audition. My grandmother ended up having to take my father along with them. At the audition, the director gave my dad and his famous sister some chocolate to share. Chocolate had been rationed at that time because of the war. My father, being very naughty, also ate my auntie's chocolate, and the director ended up giving the role to my dad! My dad said he felt amazing and felt incredible for it, but he also ended up getting bullied at school because of it.

He felt good, and the other kids were jealous. It's important to always stay humble—not for others, but because when you're on set, you're just doing a job. Unfortunately, some people react with jealousy instead of celebrating someone else's success. That's why it's crucial to have a positive support network around you to help you keep going. Letting others' jealousy bring you down will only hinder your path to success.

Being so close to someone who had already experienced success helped me add to my knowledge. I had seen it first-hand. Not only had my dad and auntie performed in films, but I had my dad telling me that anything is possible, and

Self-Knowing

I can do whatever I want to in life. Being told that at such a young impressionable age is exactly what helped me to achieve the success that I have today.

Self-knowing is where we get confidence from. Not cocky, arrogant, egocentric fake confidence that can hold us back, but confidence that holds us correctly and gives us a sense of stability, calmness, and peace.

Chapter 3
Mistakes to Avoid: Part 1

It is of the utmost importance to avoid making the mistake of letting your ego run the show, as with any job and most situations in life.

I have covered a lot on the ego in the "Ego" chapter. Make sure you give it a thorough read.

I explain in another chapter that I was always extremely anxious, even when applying for castings and different roles. Deep down, I had low self-esteem, was painfully shy, and didn't feel good about the world around me due to past experiences.

I always knew that if I acted happy, bubbly, and energetic and beamed my smile at everyone, I could make friends. I always knew when the shoot, had finished, I would never

Mistakes to Avoid: Part 1

see any of them again, and so what if I made a fool of myself? So, what if no one liked me? It didn't matter, I was there for the experience and to do my best to shine and stand out, using the knowledge I did have about performing to the best of my ability. If I did make a friend, what a bonus that would be!

The very first on-set experience that I had was a beach party scene. Not only did I meet a guy who told me he was also on Star Now, but at the end of the shoot when everyone was ready to go home, the guy who was pretending to be the DJ came and spoke to me. I will give him the name, "Justin," as I can't use his real name for obvious reasons. I also mention him in my other book with more detail about this story, "Sex, Good or Bad?" The full story isn't needed for the main point of this book.

I thought he was another extra, with a slightly better role. He was placed right at the back from where the cameras were, which were placed at the front with the lead solo artist, and us dancers were infront of him and behind the lead solo artist.

During my time dancing on set, there was a moment where I tripped over a wire while dancing and not paying attention. I was in another world, pretending no one could see me and having a wonderful time feeling free.

Suddenly I was mortified, and the quickest thing I could think of to not look like a complete idiot was to pretend I was drunk. At least I managed to numb the mortification. It didn't matter what anyone thought of me. The shoot would end, and I wouldn't ever see anyone ever again.

Of course, I wasn't drunk, and looking back on this, Justin came over to ask me if I was drunk. I was extremely good at acting, and this makes me smile on the inside.

At the end of the shoot, Justin came to speak to me, I felt extremely nervous but also excited.

At the time, I forgot that I had seen him hovering in the doorway with other crew members while practicing the beach party dance. I saw him looking at me, and I felt excited then, but had to quickly dismiss it and not focus on it. Whenever I was in awe of a guy I was seeing, I mistook it for love—but it wasn't. Whenever that feeling came up, I had to push it away. The nervous excitement was a sign that, deep down, I knew the truth. I had to remind myself that he was just another extra in the scene, so I could ask him to play certain music and tunes as part of the act, making it more fun for both of us. Looking back at that moment when I asked him to play a song, it was quite funny. I always wondered if he knew what I wanted to say, but refused to say.

I said, "I don't like this song, can you change it please?" He asked me what I wanted, to which I replied with the first artist I could think of "Rihanna". He then asked me which one. The first song that came to my mind was S&M. I couldn't say the name of the song out loud to him, and the thought of doing so absolutely mortified me.

Mistakes to Avoid: Part 1

"Quick! Think of another! Any song of Rihanna's, just not that one." I thought.

I was desperately trying to think of a different song while overacting placing an index finger on my top lip and looking up and to the side with my eyes. While I was trying to think of a different song, I made sure that I communicated to him that I was still thinking. Yet, the song title I wanted to keep in my private thoughts wouldn't leave my head. "Any song! Not that one!" I felt so embarrassed. I didn't feel safe having that as my first thought as I was trying to stay away from men. I thought that anything to do with sex might make them think I was leading them on.

The guy from Star Now saved the day, "We found love in a hopeless place". Oh my God, I was so relieved, and I reckon it showed on my face too. To get far away from that moment, the other guy and I started singing and dancing along to the Rihanna song now playing in our heads, returning to the fun, happy, and excited version of myself. One of the first things Justin said to me was, "What is your name?"

I was acting in film mode and still on a high from being on a real film set. I wanted to play and have fun and assumed everyone that was there loved films, and knew lots of words to many films, I thought it would be fun to enact one out.

The film Pretty Woman came to my mind where Vivian played by Julia Roberts asks Edward played by Richard Gere, "What do you want it to be?" That was after he asked her for her name.

"What do you want it to be?" I said it in the same flirtatious way that Julia Roberts did.

Justin scoffed not impressed at my response.

"OH NO! He doesn't get it!" Another awkward and embarrassing moment was had.

I quickly said the next line from the movie using my own name, "Frankie, my name is Frankie!"

Justin looked at me, seemingly confused, as if he recognized the lines I was saying. Could he tell I was acting? But I didn't care—I knew I'd soon be on a train, far away from all these people, never to see any of them again.".

I thought he wouldn't ask me any more questions, which was fine. I wasn't attached to him.

He did ask me more questions, "What do you do?"

I always hated that question. The truth, which isn't the truth anymore, is "single mum on benefits" and the answer I did give is more the truth now, but back then it was hardly ever.

Awkwardly, and feeling like a liar, "I am a writer."

"What do you write?"

Also hating more questions,

"Poems, articles, short stories", I was desperately trying to think of lots of different things to say to sound like I was a busy writer who was perhaps paid for their work.

Mistakes to Avoid: Part 1

"Have you ever written any film scripts?"

At the same time that I was about to say "no" I remembered that I had started to try and write a film script.

His question made me stop in my tracks because, at that time, I believed it wasn't common to have that in one's mind. I believed it was rare. Yet he asked me about writing a film.

I looked at him curiously like I had felt seen. I suddenly wanted to know more about why he asked me that question. I didn't have the words to say to him that I wanted to say. That must be part of my Asperger's syndrome. (Asperger's Syndrome isn't used as a diagnosis anymore, and I don't like it. From now on I will use "Autism"). I have never heard someone say, "Why have you asked me that question?" It isn't common. I might start using it. It certainly feels like a protective barrier, but it would also in the situation I was in, let him answer my question, which he was dying for me to ask.

I wasn't sure if the reason he was talking to me was to get my phone number. Guys that speak to me often ask me for my phone number.

I was shocked and a little confused when he asked me for my email address, that was something different, but, I also didn't see the point. I wondered if he was just being polite and getting out of asking for my number because he was never planning to call me.

I am also wondering now if it was part of his seduction plan to capture my attention. (You can read in more detail in my other book on the psychology behind it, "Sex, Good or Bad?")

I gave him my email address, never expecting to hear from him again.

Two weeks or so later, after forgetting about my interaction with him, I had an email pop up in my inbox, from someone I had never heard of. I guessed it was junk mail or spam, and as I was about to delete it without opening it, but just before clicking "delete," I noticed a yellow star next to it, labelling it as important.

The email caught my attention, so I decided to open it.

I couldn't believe it when I read it. It was Justin from my first-ever experience on set. It was even more amazing than I could have ever imagined. He told me he was an award-winning film director and writes his material and he is keen to read other people's scripts.

At this point in my life, my self-esteem was very low, and I always looked up to other people and felt that everyone else around me was better than me; so, you might be able to imagine the feeling of total awe that I had for him. It made me feel afraid. I knew in the past this feeling for men had gotten me into trouble, so I made sure that I would never meet him unless it was for business.

Mistakes to Avoid: Part 1

When I saw Justin's name from the email, I decided to find him on Facebook. I also put his name into Google and found some pictures of him with an award and of the agent he was with.

I was so excited when I found him on Facebook and felt so shy and awkward clicking "add friend".

"Who the hell was I to him?" I thought. "What could I possibly do for him to make him interested in me?" To me, he was a massive celebrity, and I was in awe of him.

A day or two later when I saw that he had accepted my friend request on Facebook, I felt my insides explode. Wow! He accepted my friend request. He acknowledged me!

I felt kind of embarrassed. I felt a bit like an imposter.

The excitement I felt about an award-winning film director emailing me and telling me he was interested in reading other people's scripts motivated me to seriously get cracking on with some work.

I never messaged him directly, but I shared with the world via my Facebook posts what I was up to. WRITING A FILM SCRIPT! Every time I struggled, I wrote a Facebook post, I wrote everything and hoped he would see it and reach out to me.

I didn't have a clue about what I was doing, I just knew I had a great story.

I wrote what I could, an outline of the whole thing.

But then when it came to writing it in script form, I found myself stuck. I realized I had no idea what I was doing.

I was scared to approach the man I viewed as a huge celebrity, but he was my only hope in being able to write my film script and technically I was doing it for him.

I couldn't believe it when he wanted my phone number to call me. I was terrified! I was so nervous. I was not the highly energetic "I don't care what anyone thinks of me" person I was while being on set.

I was so embarrassed and felt so shy, but it felt a little bit like love. I put the love onto him rather than knowing the love was me. (You can read more about "what we see in others is a reflection of ourselves" in my book "Sex, Good or Bad?").

I sent him my outline of the story which was terrifying because of the content and now I see that was probably a big mistake. We had another phone call where I felt even worse but even more in awe that he still wanted to talk to me after reading my film script idea.

I couldn't believe it. He didn't hate me or think I was disgusting after reading what he read. Wow!

He told me about the screenwriting software needed. Celtx is a free one, but I knew I needed Final Draft if I wanted to be professional. Justin also recommended a book for me to read on screenwriting.

Mistakes to Avoid: Part 1

I loved that he was talking to me. I had him high up on the highest pedestal. Even though I had him high up, I still knew he was nowhere near my ultimate dream. The place most actors and actresses dream of is Hollywood.

Where I was then, no way I could have coped acting alongside A-list actors and film directors. So, even though this story was a mistake I could have avoided, it was still a huge learning stepping stone for me, which I will discuss in another chapter.

During the next few months, I focused solely on writing my screenplay in the hope that Justin would love it and want to direct it. Looking back that was a silly thing to think, but I had my hopes and dreams of making it big in the film industry, whether that was acting or scriptwriting.

I loved the excitement of having my script to focus on and also knowing Justin was just an easy message away, whether it was email, Facebook, or now mobile messaging. I knew there was a possibility that my dream wouldn't come to fruition, but I had to try.

I knew the saying "It's not what you know but who you know!"

I worked every day trying to figure out how to write my film script. There were lots of different ways to do it. I also felt my confidence shrink as I knew Justin had been to film school, and I had never even heard of film school. I wasn't sure how films were made; I just thought someone out there with a big pot of money made them. I was fascinated to learn something new.

Also, during the next few months, I learned that Justin had directed three episodes of a long-running daytime TV soap. I watched all three episodes and felt the excitement rush through me as his name came up in big letters across the screen. This clarified to me that he was a genuine big-film director in the industry. I couldn't believe my luck!

I still only had to focus on my work though, as the saying goes, "You should never mix business with pleasure".

I first met Justin in June and by December we somehow started talking a bit more regularly. He most definitely would have approached me first, as there was no way I was going to approach him until I had finished writing my film script. I needed a good reason to message him.

I guess he knew this and when he suggested meeting up, I just assumed it was to do with my film script, or, in my head I made it about that as I didn't believe he could ever be meeting me for pleasure. What would an amazing high-up film director celebrity want with me?

Of course, those reading this, will possibly already know the answer. My naïve self couldn't see it or didn't want to take responsibility for it, yet my unworthy low self-esteem hoped it might be.

I was flattered by his attention and couldn't believe he might actually fancy me and want a relationship. It was never

Mistakes to Avoid: Part 1

truly a relationship, but my low self-worth, which was in awe of him, kept me stuck. I also held onto the hope that one day he might cast me in a film, and I could become a proper actress. The mistake I made was putting him on a pedestal so high and my feeling of being so inadequate compared to him. Falling for his flattery and attention was a huge mistake. The mistake I made was relying on him and not properly believing in myself. I made the mistake of procrastinating and hoping someone else would make my dream come true.

No one can make your dream of becoming an actor come true, but you and the effort you put in, can. You are already that superstar you know you can be, and viewing others in the industry as shining better than you and needing their attention is a huge mistake. You must always focus on shining the bright light that comes from inside of you. The superstar you see in others is your reflection of your superstardom.

Chapter 4
Theatre acting vs film and TV

Theatre acting is big and over the top so the people at the back of the audience watching can see and know what is going on.

Although I haven't made it to RADA yet, I did meet Richard. He is an award-winning film director and he learnt everything he knows from there., Richard gave me some valuable tips:

- Less is more when acting for TV.
- Film yourself performing a scene the way you envision it, then film it again with less effort. Continue scaling it down each time, and compare to see which version looks best.

He even came to watch me at some weird tacky on-stage show I did. I had an audition for a role in a TV series (that

Theatre acting vs film and TV

was the casting call description) and I got the role. I was over the moon and then they decided they wanted to do a stage show. I was terrified but embarrassingly went with it, even though it felt very strange and not legitimate. "Just in case" it is real, I went with it. I succeeded. Even though it didn't get me onto a TV series, I still had the experience of an audition and the experience of being on stage just adding to my experience of acting. It was terrifying but also kind of fun.

After he came to see me, he said I needed to be louder. I have always known that I need to be louder, I have been told many times and I always told myself I couldn't do theatre. He said that I should speak in a higher pitch so it is louder. I embarrassingly thought he meant to throw my voice, which I gave my best shot at. He told me, "No, that is throwing your voice, speak higher." I was happy that I succeeded in throwing my voice but mortified I had gotten it wrong. I am a good ego deflator and can cover it up well. That is also why I can be a good actor. If you feel embarrassed or mortified when performing, you must never let it show. Negative feelings are always from the ego.

The great thing about film and TV acting is that they give you a little microphone to hide within the costumes/clothes you wear. I am always so thrilled when I get to have that experience. Getting the proper experience of a real actor or actress. My goal is to get regular acting roles where I always get to have a microphone attached to me. Although sometimes it is like a bearskin, the tall black fury hats that some of the royal guards wear around Buckingham Palace. They hold the bearskin-looking thing on a pole and above the actor's head, out of shot/ sight of the camera.

With both acting and theatre, you have to repeat your performance over and over again which can get tedious and boring. With theatre, you do the same show many times all the way just once. With film and TV, you do the same scene over and over again. What I love about film and TV is that once the scene is done, however many times, it is finished, forever. You never have to perform it again. Unless actors pull out or some other reason. You also get to see your performance, which more often than not you can't always do with theatre.

Chapter 5

Headshots

If you have the money to spend and want to get into acting with good professional headshots, then I recommend A. P. Wilding. She does all my headshots now, and the quality is incredible. She knows what casting directors look for, knows your best angles, and can make everyone go, "Wow!"

I have known many people in the industry who got roped into spending so much money on their first "professional" photographs, but they were not proper headshots, not the industry standard that casting directors want to see. They may as well have done their research and given their money to a top-quality industry professional, like A. P. Wilding. A. P. Wilding is also recommended on Spotlight. So, when you upload your headshots, it is made easy as she comes up in the selection box. She has even won awards for her amazing work!

F.G. Fraser

If you're not in a position to spend a lot of money, you can get Time for Print (TFP) headshots where you give your time for free, and the photographer gives their time for free, and you both get photos for a portfolio, but you must know what casting directors look for, so you can guide the photographer as best as possible.

When you have a photographer and you have the date set up, you need to prepare yourself for the photo shoot. Get plenty of sleep, start drinking a lot more water, and try to stick to the new habit as much as possible, your health and skin will thank you. You must use only a minimum amount of make-up. Just a little bit of light foundation and some mascara; if you have great skin, you can go without completely like A. P. Wilding always says about me. However, I always prefer my photos with a little foundation. I am confident to go without for now for some of the beginning shots. If that is what casting directors like to see, so be it!

I only ever wear a small amount of make-up, even when I put on a full face. With my first photos, I did have a full face of make-up, but I hardly put any on anyway, so I got away with it, all my pics had the same make-up on as the first.

For your main headshot, a neutral pose is best- no smiling or only a very slight smile; just be relaxed and show your authentic self through your eyes. Nothing else apart from your head and shoulders must be shown. Do not have your hands on your face, just natural, neutral head and shoulders. A striking clear photo of just YOU!

Headshots

Choose a maximum of five different outfits that could play a different character or set a different mood for the shot.

An idea for each could be . . .

1. A plain black top or a casual hoody with a depressed expression and no make-up
2. A white top with minimal make-up and a neutral expression
3. A bright colour top with a bright friendly welcoming smile - you can do a little bit more make-up.
4. You can add a bit more make-up to this one, choose another style top, maybe wear glasses if you have them, and strike a look at how you feel.
5. This one you can add even more make-up but still very subtle and not too much, choose a sexy dress, perhaps a lower-cut top, and look like you want to kill someone.

After my very first photo shoot with a friend who was a photographer, a casting director told me that one of my photos was a very good headshot. A casting director was very impressed with it. I will add it on the next page so you can see. The photo was taken by Bruce Inman.

The shirt I am wearing is a blue and red colour,
with orange and the jacket is bright red.

The next photograph below is where I succeeded in getting a role for a music video and other roles.

The dress I am wearing is a bright and
bold peachy pink colour.

From the same photo shoot with A. P. Wilding, we got the following shots. Each shot was something slightly different, but all me. Acting is all through the eyes. The previous shot was when she asked me to do something that felt like being "me."

The next shot I was asked to do a sexy shot. A. P. Wilding said that male photographers would ask me to look sexy, something she doesn't, and rather, she asked me to look like I want to kill someone.

I wore a gold-coloured dress for this shot.

When you have a few shots taken, you can have one smiley one that is your smile, but never use it for the main shot, the first shot that casting directors will see; just have it there so they can see your smiley personality.

F.G. Fraser

This is the same bright, bold peachy pink colour. A. P. Wilding didn't know why I wanted both images from the selection. This one is smiley, and the other one isn't.

The next 2 shots I can't remember the thought behind the eyes, but the one in the thin white jumper and an interesting neckline, was said to be good for a period-type drama, and the photo with the yellow vest top was the first photo we did, and it was for the "girl next door" character look.

You will need to update your headshots every year or every 2 years for an adult and every 6 months for a child.

Headshots

Before my 2nd headshot session with A. P. Wilding, I went and had another session with a different photographer, free of charge. I went with my actor friend for him to also have a photoshoot as he had a story in a magazine and needed to have a photo alongside it.

For some reason or another, we exchanged phone numbers, and he saw my current headshot done by A. P. Wilding. He thought it was really good, and he offered me a free photo shoot. I think he wanted to practice getting some decent headshots for his portfolio.

However, the photos didn't come out so well. The thing with me is that I don't have much self-esteem or confidence, and it is difficult to believe the photographs from A. P. Wilding were me. I had gained weight since I had the photoshoot and always felt like a fraudster for using them, so I wanted new ones done.

But the ones by A. P. Wilding are always incredibly amazing, and most definitely me!

He gave me four of them free of charge in total.

The not-so-great images were the following . . .

F.G. Fraser

In the last of these headshots, the photographer
said, "Imagine you're a bear coming out of a cave."
A. P. Wilding said she had never heard of that before,
and as you can see, I look a bit "weird."

The lighting in the ones with the black top on is far too dark; you can't see me very clearly at all! In the "non-bear out

Headshots

of a cave shot," I do like the neutral and relaxed expression on my face.

I don't like to slate someone else's work, but you can see they are not my best photos. I am glad I didn't pay for them.

The following headshots were also taken by A. P. Wilding. I remember the first photo-shoot I did. I managed to lose some weight for it, not thinking I wouldn't be able to keep the weight off. So, then I gained it back again. This is a huge mistake. Do NOT try to lose weight. Go at a comfortable weight, eating healthily. There are so many acting roles out there, and you don't need to be super thin. I braved it and went for a photo shoot with A. P. Wilding with more weight on me. I wasn't keen on my non-A. P. Wilding shots. I wasn't confident because of my weight, and I wasn't confident with him either.

The top I am wearing is black.

F.G. Fraser

I am wearing a thin pastel blue and white jumper.

This was a long, white, flowing dress.

Headshots

A black satin vest top with a bright pink jacket. I had some stunning images from this set of images in this outfit and A. P. Wilding couldn't understand why I chose this one. It is because I had a big smile in the other one, and this smile was different. I do regret not getting one of the other smiley images. I did look amazing in it. If you love a photo, use it!

This was a dark red dress.
More like the colour maroon.

The previous photo of me with the sexy "I want to kill someone" look, was attached to the fire-fighter costume I wore when I got a role as a background artist. So, I am guessing this was the casting team's favourite shot of me.

Each photo shoot I had with A. P. Wilding, I was a lot more confident than the last, and I knew what to expect.

The next photo shoot I had with her, A. P. Wilding said it was my best work yet.

My T-shirt was a light orange. I wore a subtle necklace for this too. A. P. Wilding said this was perfect for a casting director casting for a soap.

Headshots

We chose a purple Pakistani top, and A. P. Wilding said it would be good for a sci-fi genre film or TV series.

I wanted a different image, perhaps a character that worked in an office, so I put a white shirt on and wore my glasses. The mood we were going for was the top one of me in the white shirt, but I loved the half-smile one and thought it might be good for a comedy or something.

F.G. Fraser

We added a bit more make-up for this. I wore a long brown dress and a long cream cardigan jacket type of thing. This photo was attached to a costume I wore for a role. I am guessing the casting team liked this headshot. However, the casting director that I met on my recent 4-week acting film course wasn't keen on this shot of me. I have never been keen on it either. Go with your gut and trust your instincts. I am looking forward to when I need to update my headshots again. I have a lot more confidence now.

This was a red lace dress, and the mood was bright, buzzy, and flirty. We added even more make-up for this shot. Still, not too much and overloaded. A bit more lipstick, and a tiny bit of brown eyeliner. More mascara. A. P. Wilding gave me a bit of eye

Headshots

shadow too. The good thing about A. P. Wilding is that she is good with make-up too. She can make you look amazing with hardly any make-up on. At my last costume fitting, I saw this smiley photo of me on the wall.

I won't add my all-time favourite photos by A. P. Wilding as they are not acting headshots. I had a creative session with her, to apply for modelling agencies. I only applied for 2. That is not how you do it. You must be hungry and apply, and apply for loads and loads.

However, one of the photos that came out was to be the perfect headshot that I love. I do have a bit more make-up on than I should for a headshot, which is probably why I love it! But also, because it has a neutral expression, and I know how I felt when I did it. Magic!

I love this, just neutrally me. I wanted to try and be sexy, a Cindy Crawford-style image. It is nothing like how I imagined, but when I did this, I felt present, and I could feel myself in the shirt.

F.G. Fraser

At my recent acting course, my tutor who is a working actor recommended two other photographers to me, Imperia Staffieri and Andrew James. I might try them one day if I fancy a change.

Chapter 6
Showreels

A good headshot is the most important thing to have rather than worrying too much about having a showreel.

A showreel isn't 100% needed, but a good showreel will get you far. Especially with background artist agencies like Talent Talks that often get acting roles that ask for a self-taped audition.

I have always been a perfectionist. I have always compared myself to other actors with amazing showreels, and the thought of just doing a self-tape showreel made me feel horrendous.

If you don't have a showreel, (I heard this from A. P. Wilding but also the staff at Talent Talks) a simple self-taped amateur showreel is fine, you can just make something up in your bedroom or living room against a plain background/ wall.

F.G. Fraser

All my showreel footage is acting roles I secured over the years and put together. If you decide on having a showreel then it shouldn't ever be longer than 2 minutes and 30 seconds. If you're a well-established actor and have scenes with famous actors, then it mustn't ever be longer than 4 minutes.

Casting directors sit through hundreds of actors and watch hundreds of showreels, they don't have time to sit through a whole showreel. They will only usually watch the first 30 seconds and decide if they want to put you through to the next round of auditions. For them to watch your whole showreel they will need to be hooked in from the beginning and not be made to watch more than a few seconds of any one scene. Perhaps you can even impress them with a variety of different characters you can perform for them to see.

It is the same with the headshot. The initial headshot needs to be a striking one to get you noticed. Casting directors review thousands of headshots, so yours must stand out immediately.

Chapter 7
Casting Websites

In November 2010, I had an opportunity to interview Beth Kingston who played India in the TV soap Hollyoaks. One of the questions I asked her was "How did you get into acting?"

Beth told me that she got onto as many casting websites as she possibly could and applied for absolutely everything that she possibly could. She also said she was very lucky that her dad paid for her to do a summer course at RADA for film and TV.

I was very nervous at this point in my life and had low self-esteem. Even just getting on a casting website filled me with anxiety. "Who am I with little experience to join a casting website? No one will ever choose me."

I googled "Casting Websites" The first casting website that came up was "Casting Now". I clicked on it and saw a list of available castings that being a member of, I could apply for.

Even though I had so many doubts and the membership fee was over £100 for the year, I called up my dad and asked him for the money. Miraculously, he did agree to pay it for me after I told him about my interaction with Beth.

I was thrilled to be on this platform and often browsed through the list of castings. I felt very nervous looking at all the auditions, doubting anyone would choose me due to my minimal experience—mostly limited to a few roles in school productions. I briefly attended a theatre school, which included dance and singing. I felt extremely self-conscious and embarrassed; I felt like I had two left feet in dance class, and during singing class, I often mimed to make it seem like I was Singing. I think the teacher caught on because she suddenly got everyone to stop singing and came over to me to get me to do a solo. I was mortified. I believed that I couldn't sing, and I was painfully shy. It felt excruciating to think that everyone's eyes were on me. I think the majority of the other students were pretty outgoing, and one of them seemed extremely extroverted and hoped the teacher would see them as being the best. Either that or they just really enjoyed singing and dancing and put tons of energy into it.

When I look back, I imagine that some of them had big dreams that both of their parents had encouraged, and supported from a very young age. That could have been my judging ego though.

Casting Websites

Whenever I eagerly looked through the list of auditions for various things I always felt too scared to apply. I sort of applied for one or two things, but I didn't get a response.

I didn't look often because I felt small and incapable. After all, I didn't think I was good enough.

After a few months of being on the website, I saw a casting for the reality TV show Big Brother. I always dreamed of being an actor, but because my dad had paid for the yearly subscription, I just knew I HAD to audition for something. It was an open audition, and you could just turn up. Auditioning for Big Brother felt a lot easier and had less risk of experiencing imposter syndrome.

I took my friend Emma with me; she didn't get past the first round. I did. I got past the second round too. I eventually had to fill in a huge, massive form with loads of questions asking all about your life in detail. It was crazy! It was fun and it felt good that someone was so interested in me and my life. I felt important for a change.

After filling out the huge form, I was taken to a mock Big Brother diary room. No fancy chair—just a regular one in front of a huge camera lens. It was so much fun! I was convinced I'd get a callback, and so were all my friends. However, we were sworn to secrecy and could only tell one other person. My friend, who had been waiting for me for ages, couldn't resist telling her friends. They all thought I'd get into the house, and when I didn't, my friend exclaimed, "I have no idea how you didn't get into the Big Brother house!"

I saw it as confidence building but also a good thing because I wanted to be an actress. I have never seen a Big Brother contestant go on to be a successful actor. Another big scary thing to grow from. I was happy that I had my friend Emma come with me and plan the train journey. I could just tag along, her being my special guide. Finding travel routes to unfamiliar places is a serious anxiety-inducing stress factor and it must be due to the Autism I have. I have a book in mind for the future. "Autism at Mainstream School: Good or Bad?" I haven't finalised the title yet, but it will be on the subject of Autism.

In the queue for the Big Brother audition. I met a lovely guy that I stayed friends with for a long time. He told me about a good casting website. It was called Star Now. He was the first one to mention Star Now to me. Before the guy, I met onset the music video in Chapter 3.

I didn't go home and sign up straight away as I was tired from the excitement of the Big Brother audition. I wasn't very good at doing things back then either. Doing anything felt like a huge hurdle. I was OK, where I was. I was hoping Big Brother would be my easy way out and I wouldn't have to do anything.

When the year's subscription had ended, it automatically took money out of my dad's account. I was pleased to have another year, but my dad wasn't, and I felt guilty, so I said I would pay my dad back in instalments, which I did.

Casting Websites

I saw a casting, "a role in a Hollywood movie with training."

"Oh my God!" I felt so excited! "This would be perfect for me! If they're giving training".

I have been told by so many people that I look stunning and have often been told I look like various A-List stars, including Scarlett Johansson. I applied feeling excited and I was even more excited when I received a reply message.

I was invited to do an acting workshop which I had to pay for. I instantly knew it was probably a bit of a scam, however, my excitement and enthusiasm for acting in films overtook my thinking it was a scam.

"I thought I would go along and see what it was all about". I will keep my wits open and be on high alert, so I don't get fully scammed.

The acting workshop was fun because I was doing what I loved. I didn't see how that would get me into a Hollywood movie though.

I was right!

One of the first things that caught my eye was the lady in charge was in a wheelchair. I thought, that if she is a scammer, then the wheelchair makes her look vulnerable. I couldn't help but not trust her, because of it.

On the same day that I was there, there was a participant who had done the workshop before. The lady in charge called her out. She complimented her but said she could do with some one-on-one training with her. I felt a bit jealous that my performance hadn't been called out on. I was desperate to be good enough for a Hollywood movie. (I am so glad my desperation has subsided!)

Anyway, in the hope that my dream might come true, I ended up paying and doing another workshop. Well, well, well, part of my performance was to be a presenter, so I did my thing.

At the end of it, the lady then called me up on my performance. She said I was being myself and not acting, (even though I had to learn a script for it and I was presenting something). She then said it was a shame because I did so much better last time at the workshop, and I had a good look. She then invited me to have a one-on-one session with her. I instantly thought if it was a lot of money then the answer would be "No!"

My answer was a "no." Two lots of forty pounds for a 3-hour workshop was plenty enough. If it looks too good to be true, then it probably is. An easy route to get into a Hollywood movie was not going to be.

I counted how many people attended the workshop and I counted loads. More than 30, possibly 40 or even 50. That is between £1200 and £2000 for 3 hours, and this was supposed to get me a role in a Hollywood movie.

Casting Websites

I felt disappointed that my Hollywood dream would not become a reality any time soon. I also felt a little pleased though that she hadn't got me caught up in her scam any longer.

The charming participant I worked with told me, after her negative comment, that he thought my performance was very good. Bless him! I liked him and will always remember the positives of my performances. Being as shy as I am and being able to perform in front of others is terrifying, but there I go and try it anyway.

"I am never going to see these people again," I always think, and all of us participants are there for the same reason.

Even though she didn't seem legit, I had fun practicing the craft I wanted to do with others and meeting new people. Not stuck at home. I had to get my mum to help me plan my route and I was terrified doing it, but I managed to do it because my acting dream was stronger than any fear. I grew up in that area too. Practicing unfamiliar journeys all alone and returning home safely, surviving.

The Big Brother auditions were on again, but earlier the next year. They ran the first Channel 5 episode in the autumn and the celebrity one in January. The auditions were earlier as the show was aired in the Summer.

I was told they could call me up at any time, even right up until the end of the show. So, I joined a good gym, started a healthy eating routine, and began to feel great in my body.

(I plan to release another book in the near future: *Diets/Fasting: Good or Bad? Why I Had a Gastric Sleeve and Is It Something You Should Consider?* —hopefully, the answer is no!)

Feeling good about myself and my body, I revisited the casting website and saw a role for a music video, though it was just a background part. I decided to apply, even though I didn't expect to hear back. I submitted my application without too much anxiety. If they called, I'd handle my emotions then. I assumed they wouldn't, but I felt strong and confident just for applying.

One day a friend asked me if I wanted to go to the gym with him and then go in the jacuzzi after. I did. I liked his company. He then came back to my place for a cup of tea.

My phone started ringing and I answered it without a clue who it might be. I certainly wasn't expecting it to be the callback. I went through the call, keeping my cool, pretending I had done this before, and I was able to do it.

When I said goodbye and hung up the phone, I screeched in excitement and terror!!

"Oh my God, Oh my God, Oh my God! I applied to be in a music video, and they want me. Oh my God, I don't think I can do it. I don't think I should do it!" I whined, totally freaking out, hoping he would get me off the hook for feeling like I did.

Casting Websites

"Yes, do it, do it! You MUST do it! Whatever you say, I don't care, you're doing it!" my friend said to me. He was very adamant that I should do it, even though I felt terrified, that I couldn't. But because he was so strong and I was used to following commands, I decided I would do it.

If I made a complete fool of myself then I could pass the blame onto him. I was also very happy and excited that I was going to do it and experience a real film set for the very first time. I had no idea what to expect. I just knew it was a beach party scene and was told to bring beach party clothes.

I just had to go with the flow and also to push through any shyness.

I worked out which London tube station I had to get to, and I also decided to attempt to use Google Maps on my phone if I were to get lost. I wasn't confident that I knew how to use Google Maps. I knew if I walked away from the train station, then I just had to make sure I remembered the same route back again.

I finally decided to turn right out of the station and then turn right again down the next road. I walked past a couple of people that looked at me and I wondered if I should ask them, but I was too scared. I kept walking and then decided to pull out my phone. "It is better to try and fail than never try at all."

If I was desperate then I had a phone number I could call, but at that time I was still very nervous.

I decided to turn around and go back to the people I walked past. I walked past them slower, looking at them, wondering again. They then asked me if I was there for the shoot, and I was super happy that I was.

I beamed my smile at them and pretended I was super confident.

They said they had wondered if I was there for the shoot the first time I walked by; because I was dressed in a bright-coloured summer dress, suitable for the beach scene.

I walked with them in the direction they took me, then opened my suitcase and laid out my outfits on a chair. Some of them were bikinis because it was a beach party scene, I felt incredibly good about my body at that point, with eating healthy and regular gym sessions.

We learned an easy dance routine from the dance choreographer, and we both recognised each other. It turned out she used to live in Tunbridge Wells, my hometown. I think she mentioned the theatre school I went to, but I couldn't quite catch her. Then she said, "Ah, no, never mind!" I do think she was perhaps the dance teacher at the theatre school I went to.

I was so enthusiastic and did the routine with loads of energy then she told the others to copy me. I felt like a superstar!

When we got on set and started filming with the singer, I was happy and dancing with everyone, doing as I was told.

Casting Websites

I caught the attention of one of the other extras. He danced enthusiastically alongside me.

We got chatting and he told me about other work he had. There was a clear image of him with a football scarf advertising something, either on a flyer or a billboard. It felt exciting hanging out with someone a little bit famous. He also asked me if I was on Star Now, and he said he was on that platform. It was the second time I had heard about Star Now, but I still hadn't gotten a profile on there yet.

After my first time on a real film set, I met a guy who turned out to be an award-winning film director. You can read about him in Chapter 3, "Mistakes to Avoid Chapter, part 1".

Anyway, along my journey of eventually signing up to Star Now and meeting other people along the way who gave me advice on various casting websites that they are on, I found other good agencies that anyone can make a profile on.

The list is as follows:

www.talenttalks.co.uk

https://uk.epcastingportal.com/login

https://www.castingcollective.co.uk/ - I am still yet to join this one.

www.mandy.com

www.backstage.com

www.starnow.com - for starting.

https://www.rachelspeople.co.uk/ - I am also yet to join this one.

https://universalextras.co.uk/

https://maddog2020casting.com/en/ - I am also yet to join this one.

Most of the above websites are for extras but you do get some featured roles with some well-paid adverts too, and opportunities for other roles. Mandy and Backstage are more for actors.

https://jackrydersessions.com - This link offers one-on-one acting coaching with a renowned actor and film director, best known for his role as Jamie Mitchell in the popular TV soap 'Eastenders.

I am sure there are probably many other websites that along with your journey of meeting people, you will learn about, like I did.

Some people pay hundreds of pounds to get a showreel, I was able to put together a showreel of bits I had done. I did a few unpaid jobs for students and other short films. I desperately needed the experience, and it was incredible. I had to audition but it was amazing to be asked even to audition.

Casting Websites

When you pay to do an acting for film course at MET film school, they give you film footage that can be used as showreel.

You pay to be taught but also accumulate showreel footage. If you're going to pay for a showreel, then pay to be taught acting by professionals.

Chapter 8
Castings/Auditions

So... you have got yourself a clear, neutral, striking headshot, applied for many castings/auditions and finally, you have excitedly been short-listed and asked by the casting director to showcase your talent to them and the film director.

You don't want to mess up at the next step!!

There are two separate ways you can be asked to audition. The first is now seen as the old-fashioned way, which is to go face to face and meet with them in person; and now that I have been successful many times with a face-to-face audition, I prefer it this way.

When I first started, I preferred it the way that is mostly used now: which is to send in a self-tape. I didn't have anyone around to judge me if I made a fool of myself, and there was a good chance I would never even see the casting director if they didn't select me. If they regretted asking me to audition and thought I was terrible and wasting their time, I wouldn't have to know.

I learned that I did get responses and it felt exciting. I felt like I did have talent and I did have a chance.

What to wear

When attending an in-person audition or filming a self-taped audition, if the character isn't obvious as to what they should wear, then wear something smart but casual and neutral.

If you can imagine something that the character would wear, like a character with a job that wears a uniform, police officer, nurse, fire-fighter, or secretary, you can dress up in full costume if it feels right. I did see a casting director on my Facebook page who gave a role to an actor who turned up in a full fire-fighter uniform. That was for a foreign film and their industry. They probably do things differently than in the UK and US film industry.

When I went for an audition for a nurse, I wore a navy-blue dress, smart but casual and I was given the role. It was probably more my talent that gave me the role, but if I had turned up in punk clothes or gothic clothes, I could imagine the audition would have been more of a failure than a success.

Wearing neutral clothes that are similar to the character's attire can help you feel more in character too.

Never wear distracting patterns or bold accessories to distract the casting director away from your acting, unless you feel it fits the character, and it isn't too over the top.

How to film a self-tape

I remember when I first started doing audition self-tapes. I didn't know any better and filmed them in portrait mode. The only acting role I got through a self-tape audition was by a lucky break and my acting talent, not because I was holding my phone portrait!

The director mentioned how blown away he was by my amazing acting, he kept ranting and raving, and it felt incredible to hear, although I wasn't sure if I should believe him!!

"Surely, it can't have been that good?" Those were my thoughts. The director did have a negative about it being in portrait and at the time I was too nervous to take anything in. I think I still filmed in portrait mode for a bit until someone made it clear that it must always be filmed in landscape mode. Landscape mode is where you hold the phone horizontally and not vertically.

For ages and ages, I filmed self-tapes holding my phone in my hand. The director who cast me through my self-tape

Castings/Auditions

audition mentioned that even though I was holding my phone and filming, my acting was just incredible. Lots of brownie points for me that day! I felt over the moon and thought my acting journey from then on would continue to be smooth and easy.

An amazing actor friend of mine, who has since moved to LA, encouraged me to buy a mobile phone tripod. Wow, it has changed my life and made filming so much simpler! When I first got it, it felt like a fun new toy. I absolutely love it! If you don't have one, I highly recommend getting a mobile phone tripod.

Also, when you film a self-tape audition, the beginning should include what's called an "ident." This is where you introduce yourself and let your personality shine. Start by saying your name, and the character you're auditioning for, and, if you have an agent, mention who they are.

For example, when I was with the Grand Talent agency, I would say, "My name is Francesca Fraser, the character I am auditioning for is (character's name) and I am with the Grand Talent agency."

Then after that, you would slowly turn your head to the left and then the right so they can see what you look like from the side, and then you would show your hands, the back and the front. Then you would perform the audition.

I never did the ident until Tracey accepted me at the Grand Talent agency, so it was a real miracle that I landed the role of Sarah, in "Interception". Thank you, Tracey, for your teachings.

I am grateful, and I can only thank God with my heart and soul, and the crazy hard mental work I put into doing it. I couldn't believe it when I got the audition, and then when I got past the first round of the audition process, I was in total disbelief that I had a real chance. I worked and worked so damn hard. I needed to know that I had done my best, and it did pay off.

It was an unpaid film shoot, but I got good showreel footage from it. When I audition for a good role, I always put that same amount of effort and energy in. It pays off!

I got good feedback from a casting director with an audition through Grand Talent. The film had an A-list actress in it. I worked hard and felt I did well. They said they were impressed, and I gave them a different take on the character. I also had to do a Scottish accent which was fun. I got a Scottish friend to say the lines for me, so I could perfect the accent. It was great fun, the positive and good feedback made it all worthwhile. Incredibly satisfying!

I went to an event organised by the staff at talent talks agency and I met the actor, Tal Profs. He gave me some incredible advice. He said to only perform the ident for commercial auditions and only for film auditions if they ask you for it. If you have a self taped audition for a film or television show and they ask for an ident, add it in at the end of the tape.

Castings/Auditions

The most important thing you can do for any audition is to always follow the instructions exactly as they give them.

You will often read in the instructions given, that if you don't send your self tape file with the correct name that they ask for, they will not view your audition tape. It is crucial that you always read everything and do everything they ask of you.

Chapter 9
Spotlight

Spotlight is an online casting website that is not easy to get onto, but is extremely necessary for professional actors.

Once you are there, they have a lot of different castings that you can apply for. If you have an agent, you click the "nudge agent" tab so that your agent can apply for you.

There are certain criteria that you must have to be able to get on there. When I joined, if I remember correctly, I needed to have four professional credits or two years of drama/theatre school training. I had four professional credits and only a little bit of theatre school training.

However, as I am writing, I just typed into Google "What are the criteria needed to get onto Spotlight?" to see if it is correct for my book, and to see if it is still the same and it gave me the following . . .

Spotlight

"At least one featured role with an equity or equivalent union contract or two contracted professional performance credits. Or have completed at least a year of full-time professional performance training equivalent to an RQF level 5 or two years of part-time training."

However, I thought once I was on Spotlight and had an agent, my acting career would take off. I thought I would get lots of auditions and succeed in getting many roles. Sadly, that hasn't happened. (YET! Keeping the self knowing!)

I have since purchased Amy Jo Berman's Acting Coaching. She was an A-list Hollywood casting director and knows exactly what casting directors want to see from an auditionee. She has helped many actors secure agents and also gets loads of auditions, which is what you need as an actor, even if you're unsuccessful. She often also has business lunches with agents. Perhaps she will be the person to recommend me to a top agent. Inshallah! (God is willing.)

Chapter 10
Getting an Agent

There are many dodgy, incompetent agents out there, many con artists wishing to charge you a fee for joining.

If agents are legitimate and can get you work, they will take a percentage of the job they get you. You will need to get your headshots and pay an amount depending on the standard you opt for. You can even get TFP (time for print) headshots, from a photographer starting in the industry. As you progress in your acting career you may want to get a top-notch photographer that knows what casting directors want in the industry. I use Alexa Wilding or A. P. Wilding. She is fabulous, friendly, funny, and always manages to get amazing images. (Read more in the "Headshots" Chapter.)

Be cautious of agents that get you to work without charging any fees. You may feel obliged to be their friend,

Getting an Agent

which can lead to an unprofessional relationship where they might stop trying to get you acting work. There are some shady characters out there. If someone warns you that an agent is untrustworthy from the beginning, that is already a red flag to stay away from them. Even more of a red flag is if the person who wants to be your agent tells you they know shady people who will do bad things for them. Run!! Focus on God, focus on YOU and the talent you know you possess.

Make sure you're not tempted to use an agent's photographer who charges a lot of money for images that may not be industry standard. If you're going to pay a lot of money, do your research into the photographer. A. P. Wilding is one of Spotlight's recommended acting headshot photographers, she has even won awards for her amazing work.

I learned from Amy Jo Berman that the best way to get an agent is to be recommended by someone else. Sending cold emails is not the way to go about it.

When you do write an email to an agent asking for representation, you must also mention many positive things about your acting skills and your career, and sound incredibly confident in your capabilities.

Even though I already knew actors with agents, and applied to a couple of them, I remember not sounding confident in my email and never even heard a reply.

When I spoke to another of my incredible actor friends, who even managed to get a little role in the famous TV soap, "Eastenders", he told me which agent he was with. Since we had both been with Simon with his illegitimate agency, (more in "Mistakes to avoid"), I felt a stronger bond with him in an acting sense. So, when I approached the agent he was with, I felt more confident and I was able to sell myself properly. I think he even mentioned that he would tell her to expect my email. I also shared my negative experience with Simon and expressed my relief that she was a female agent.

She did mention that my Spotlight didn't have much to it. I told her that I had only just joined Spotlight and hadn't got around to finishing it. I added my relevant skills to Spotlight, and she said it looked much better and then accepted me. I felt relieved like I could relax. I thought I would get many more auditions than I did, but unfortunately, I didn't.

I am going to look for a new agent now as she has since closed her agency.

Being referred to an agent by someone else, also worked for me when Simon was trying to get the feature role for his new model/actor love interest that he had signed to his agency.

I was also in the photo that he showed to the casting director, Lemar, and it turned out he was interested in me. Simon then told him what an amazing actress I was and

Getting an Agent

showed him some of the self-tapes I had sent him for his feedback, as I was always worried, they were never good enough, He never told me they were bad. Looking back, I think he could have given me some constructive criticism.

Chapter 11
Let go of Desperation

If you have read my book "Sex; Good or Bad?" then you will have already read this chapter about the time I had that can only be described as a Godly experience, or Heaven, maybe Nirvana. (There is a part in the Quran that mentions seeing a light and then being shown the holy book.)

To cut this chapter short, I desperately wanted the heavenly experience to fill every cell of my body. Instead of letting it be, I tried to grab hold of it, gripping it tightly in my desperation to want more of it. As soon as I did this, the most incredible life experience I had ever had – and was incomparable to anything in this physical world - shut off and stopped.

The intense desire to succeed as an actor is something many of us share, but it's important to let things unfold naturally. Enjoy every moment, but loosen your grip and avoid attaching

Let go of Desperation

too much meaning to any single event on your acting journey. Take the necessary steps with faith and belief, then let go and avoid feeling disappointed. Your determination should be focused on the hard work you put into perfecting your performance, not on whether you get the role. Remember, acting is all about being in the present moment.

I hope you enjoy reading my story. The film director I mentioned is the same one who once had me excited and I put him on a pedestal. You'll find more about that in Chapter 3: "Mistakes to Avoid."

My Heavenly Experience

In June 2012, the first time I was on set, an award-winning film director took an interest in me. I thought he was just another extra, like me, but his friend was the director and had asked him to help on set, so he did.

I didn't know he was a film director until he emailed me a few days later and said he was interested in other people's scripts and stories. I got excited and started writing my film script.

While I was writing the film script based on my true-life events, I realised I had a lot of pain and shame in me.

I went to the deepest part of me, which connects to who some call God and others Allah, some may have different names.

I vowed never to drink alcohol again, eat pork, or have sex unless it was with a man I was married to. I felt the shame and the pain and vowed to never have a sinful thought again. In everything I did, I held onto God. It was a lonely path to be on. I didn't see many people, only my son.

I felt purified, though I was unfamiliar with many practices like praying five times a day. I knew about Ramadan, abstaining from alcohol, and the basics of being a good person.

I decided to get a discreet tattoo to mark the occasion, as I had always been curious about having one but didn't think a visible tattoo would suit me.

I wore a scarf for a few days, finding comfort in being hidden from view. It made me feel secure, shielded from unwanted attention and catcalls on the street.

I felt embarrassed because I didn't know anyone else who wore a head scarf, leaving me feeling isolated. This led me to only last a couple of days fully covered.

I decided to end my script idea with a tattoo and included it in the outline I sent to the film director.

I felt refreshed and serene, focusing on pure thoughts. However, after a few months, I found myself craving connection.

Let go of Desperation

I joined the Plenty of Fish dating site and went on a few dates. I refused to let any man get too close to me though. Even if they were lovely and fanciable.

One of the guys I spoke to on Plenty of Fish was handsome. I felt weak and I didn't trust myself.

I also felt a lot of shame when reading the part of his profile that said he didn't like promiscuous women. I believed I had no chance with him at all and I felt very timid even messaging him!

We were chatting and sending each other messages. He suggested we become Facebook friends. He also told me about his Mum being a Reiki healer and having a group on Facebook, that I joined.

I got chatting with his Mum and she mentioned she had a free meet-up group planned. Now, because I fancied her son, this was a huge motivator to get me to travel to his flat in London to see his Mum, and have the Reiki session. I was more interested in having the Reiki session, but the excitement that I might see her son made it much more interesting.

I wasn't very good at planning my train route and I ended up going a super long way round and ended up getting there when the group finished. There was only one other lady who had attended the group, and she had a one-to-one with the handsome man's mother before I arrived.

It was raining hard, and I turned up soaking wet. I was super excited to meet his mystical mother who could give me some healing. She opened the door, and I shone my beaming smile at her. She said because there were only 2 of us and I had turned up late, we could have a one-to-one session. "It is meant to be and it is important for you both," She said.

After she put my socks on the radiator to dry out, she made me a cup of tea and had a chat. I told her about the film director and immediately she had bad vibes and told me to stay away from him.

Then we started to get into it. She asked me to pick a card out from a pack facing downwards. I chose the Magic card.

"Ooo, the magic card!" She said with mystery, while I remember watching my wet socks drying on the radiator.

She told me I would experience some magic within the next couple of days. I had already experienced what I would call a miracle, so I just brushed it off believing it would be similar to that. However, I still felt positive because it was always a fantastic experience, and confirming that God has my back.

When we meditated, I was told to have my feet on the ground and to close my eyes.

She said the following as I listened and followed what she said.

Let go of Desperation

"Imagine a soft warm golden light being poured through the top of your head . . . it is so beautiful. Imagine it coming down and through your head and past your ears . . . (pause) It gets even more beautiful as it comes down . . . "

Then there was a longer pause.

I imagined this beautiful light coming down and into my stomach, I imagined it coming down.

Suddenly, Sue spoke again, "Now imagine the light coming down your throat. It gets even more beautiful as it comes down."

When she spoke, I felt interrupted and took the light back up to my throat so I could follow Sue's words properly again. I even opened my eyes to look at her. I had come out of the meditation. I had been interrupted

I then followed Sue's words the best I could until the end of the meditation.

"Now imagine the light coming down your chest, it is so beautiful. It is coming further down now. Into your stomach Wow! The light is spectacular! There are so many sparkles and whooshing beauty. Wow! It is stunning!"

I did my best to follow her, but the interruption ruined it for me.

I can't remember what happened next, but I stayed a little longer with Sue until she had finished her work with me.

The magic that I experienced a couple of nights later was nothing like what I had expected. I had no idea an experience like this could be had while on planet Earth.

I was asleep in my bed, but it wasn't a dream. It was real.

No words will ever be able to describe the experience. Words are from the mind, taken from the physical 3D reality world we all live in. This was something the mind would never be able to comprehend. But even these words cannot explain it, because still, the mind is trying to interpret them into something it can understand.

I will try and explain this experience as closely as I possibly can in words that come to my mind.

Completely out of nowhere, my usual sleep reality changed.

I didn't know I was asleep when a tiny spec of light caught hold of my awareness and attention. I looked at it curiously; it was new, something to be discovered. I can't say that I was looking at it because I had no choice. It was just there. My 3D eyes weren't open to look at it. It was from the inside.

I stayed asleep, and very gently, smoothly, softly, elegantly, the light trickled closer towards my awareness as if it was far away to begin with.

I suppose I could say this light was growing bigger and expanding. I suppose I could see it differently in that my awareness was going towards it. Wow! I have never seen

Let go of Desperation

it like that before. Always the other way, because the other way is closer to Sue's words. That is what my mind knows and tries to explain.

I hate using words to describe it, it is a memory from the past, over a decade ago. November 2012. What I experienced was there in the present moment.

I must continue; the light got bigger, or it trickled into my awareness more and more - the closer it came to me and the more of it I experienced, I saw how incredibly beautiful it was and it made me feel in an incredibly beautiful way.

My mind hadn't butted in, the light was just there, and I started to feel in awe, but unless you experience it, you won't understand the word "awe".

It was so beautiful; it was warm, and it was golden. But those words cannot explain it. Those are still words from the mind, and all words taint it. It can never be tainted. That is why there are no words to truly describe it. You wouldn't want to describe it either. You just want to experience it.

The light trickled further, and it grew more and more intensely not tense. It was so overbearingly powerful, but it was so soft and gentle. There are no words to describe the beauty I experienced.

I had never experienced such heaven on earth before.

A voice inside me butted in, "Oh Wow! What is that?" I guess, if my awareness expanded up into the light, the voice may have come from below me. Come from my body, which I was still connected to.

Then my mind was disturbed. Instead of staying still and appreciating every single blissful moment, it remembered my meeting with Sue, the magic card I had pulled out, and the meditation we did.

I remembered how, when the light descended further into my stomach, it became even more amazing and beautiful.

My mind craved this light; it wanted this heavenly beauty to permeate all corners of its existence. It was so beautiful.

I tried to grasp it. I was greedy for this light and I wanted it all at once to permeate my insides quickly.

The very moment I tried to seize it, and my mind attempted to take control, it disappeared so quickly. In an instant flash, it was gone. I was left in empty darkness.

I then woke up in my bed. I was in darkness. All I knew that what I had experienced was, that it was God, heaven, Nirvana. I was in awe, admiration, and wonder.

I sat up in my bed, still. Afraid to move, afraid to lose the moment. I was in shock too, the gentle kind of shock. That was all I had ever truly wanted and craved intently. Tears gently fell from my eyes and peacefully rolled down my cheeks.

Let go of Desperation

When I was 12, I had a beautiful holiday in the Maldives. I always called that heaven on earth. After experiencing a tiny glimpse of the true meaning of heaven, the Maldives holiday was nothing in comparison.

I believe that my decision to remain pure and disconnected from all men and what religions describe as "sin" allowed me to experience a glimpse of heaven's purity when I went to Sue.

When you truly nail a role during a performance, there's an intense lightness that lifts any heaviness from you—it feels magical. This might be why so many people dream of this profession and are so hungry for it. But if you can let go of that desperation and hunger, you'll open yourself to miracles. You'll be able to apply for roles with ease and experience true success.

Chapter 12
Mistakes to Avoid: Part 2

Remember Justin from Chapter 3?

I managed to detach myself from Justin after 2 years and 4 months. I didn't realise it at the time, but he was abusing me. (You can read more in my book "Sex, Good or Bad?")

Deep down, I had known for a very long time something wasn't right, but I couldn't get Justin to leave. I didn't know anything about narcissists until after I got rid of him. I did something I knew would make him leave forever, even though a part of me believed I desperately needed him. The part that needed him gone was stronger.

I had made a video of him on the bus to Amsterdam when he was asleep. (This was a different Amsterdam trip

Mistakes to Avoid: Part 2

to the one I tell the story of in my first book, Sex: Good or Bad?) Once, when I took a photo of Justin, he got angry and demanded that I delete it. I never took another photo of him ever again; however, he often took many photos of me that he never sent to me. I can't help but wonder if he ever sent them to anyone else, especially if you learn of the shocking detail about him that I share in my book "Sex Good or Bad?" I also wonder if he was using his camera for anything else!?!

When I felt upset by him and determined to know who else he was seeing, I spent a few hours, going well into the early morning, sending the video of us on the bus to all the women on his Facebook and some selected men.

I didn't get any clear answers. Some messaged me back. I probably told them my story and then I probably got blocked. I didn't care. I went into a very low place after I met Justin, it was the worst agonising pain. I was in pain seeing him, and the pain to release the attachment was insane. I kept emailing him long messages. I even ended up creating a new email address to contact him.

I tried so hard to stay away from emailing him. Eventually, I was able to, I didn't want to get arrested for being a stalker or harassing him. Also, I knew it wasn't good for my self-worth, to chase a man.

I Googled "how to get revenge". I then put his email address into loads of spam, and junk websites, including the most hilarious one I thought of, "How to be a good man?" A coaching series. I still giggle about that one now.

F.G. Fraser

I realise now, that a man has to want to be good, and even though I don't like to believe it, I have been forced to learn that there are many bad men in the world. I have also taught myself that there are a million more decent men out there.

When I knew the end was near to the painful "situationship" I was in with Justin, I started applying for more roles on Star Now.

I also decided that after my experiences on set as an unpaid background artist, I would attempt to go for some unpaid acting roles. No one had to know I was auditioning apart from the casting team. I thought I would give it a go.

The first audition I had was advertised for being filmed in New York, expenses paid, and earning £300 a day.

I was super excited at the thought of this prospect. I practiced and practiced and practiced. I also had to do an American accent, which I pulled off. I didn't think I would hear back, especially when I found an actress on YouTube sharing her audition which was for the same role I applied for. She was brilliant, her acting was amazing. She told me they were looking for someone with a different look even though they liked her acting.

They hadn't even replied to me, so I guessed my audition was awful. However, I was even more excited when I received an email asking for my height. Around this time, I was doing an acting for a film course and my tutor said it sounded like I was in the running for it.

Mistakes to Avoid: Part 2

I couldn't believe it! This was my first-ever audition and I was in the running. I always heard that actors and actresses have loads of auditions and get turned away, a lot, before being successful.

My second audition was a face-to-face audition at a film school for some students. I couldn't believe it when I got the role. My second audition was my first face-to-face audition, and I was successful. This showed that I had the talent, and if I kept pushing myself, eventually I would get a good role somewhere and be very well paid.

When I went to the rehearsal for my first-ever lead role, I couldn't perform like I did in the audition. When I went home, I was so ashamed and knew that somehow, I had to make myself perform. I knew that I had to be in the present moment to do it. I thought that if I drank a bottle of wine, I would forget about the rehearsal and get into the present moment. However, being so desperate that resorting to alcohol, there is no way it would work. Being present means not being desperate to do it, but just being and having no thoughts. Desperation means you don't believe you can do it.

Being hungover and a bit numb means you can't feel the emotions needed to come through your eyes. So, never, think drinking alcohol will help you. That was a huge mistake I made!

I remember freaking out over the scene in the hospital. I was desperate to get into character and be how I was when

I did it in the audition room. I kept going into the toilet to do the crazy warming-up techniques that I learned in the acting course. Looking back, I should have done the warming-up technique in front of others, then I would have felt exactly how I needed to feel to get into character. Stupid idiot and terrified, forcing myself far away from others and reality. Lesson learned for next time if I ever experience difficulty!

During my time on set, I didn't see myself as any bigger or better than anyone else, not even the extras. No one was below me.

As far as I was concerned, I was the imposter, and I somehow managed to fool the students in the audition room. Even though parts of shooting some of the scenes were scary and stressful, I loved every bit of it. I knew I had to get it just right, so my showreel looked like I was an amazing actress that knew exactly what I was doing.

When we had finished filming, I went home, and a day or so later one of the extras from onset sent me a friend request. I recognised his picture straight away and had completely forgotten his name was Simon.

"How sweet, I thought!" He thought about me and wanted to be my Facebook friend. I didn't think of him at all, as I had focused on doing my job. I had done my job and gone home. I thought it was sweet, as he must have looked up to me as the lead actress in a film that he was an

Mistakes to Avoid: Part 2

extra in. I remember looking up to the actors when I was doing unpaid background artist work. "One day I will be where you are."

When I finished shooting the student film, I felt so burnt out, even more than when I did background artist work. Whenever I did a film shoot, I always waited a while before being able to apply for another role.

During my rest time, I would often find myself on Facebook. Whenever I saw someone who was in pain, I couldn't help but leave them a nice comment to lift their spirits and hopefully make them feel better.

One day, scrolling through, I noticed it was Simon's turn with a heartbroken post, complaining about how someone had done him over and hurt him. With my wide-open heart, I left him a heartfelt message of love. Not a romantic love, but love for all humans, and the inability to bear the thought of anyone in pain. The next thing I knew, I had an inbox message from Simon. He told me he had many good connections in the industry and knew a lot of people. He said he could help me. He gave me his number and told me to call him. I get nervous calling people, especially new people, so I decided to give him my number instead.

He called me almost instantly and we had a conversation. He called me a few more times after that. I didn't have many friends call me and it was nice to have some company on the phone, even if he did sound a bit odd.

I wasn't 100% sure that I trusted everything he said, as it all sounded too good to be true. I didn't want to completely shut him down, though, just in case.

He used to say things on the phone that sounded creepy, like "Loyalty is very important to me! If anyone ever stabs me in the back, I know bad people who will do bad things for me."

This was such a huge red flag, and I should have leapt away there and then, but I didn't. I would show him that I was loyal, and a very good friend, even if he did give me the creeps. If someone gives you the creeps from the beginning, it is probably in the best interest of you both to keep away, however good their words may sound.

One of the things he repeatedly said to me was, "I am not like other men! I don't try it on—I'm the opposite." These words made him seem safe. Even though I never truly felt safe around him, I wanted to believe in that safety. He was very different from Justin. In that aspect, he felt like a huge relief.

"It's not what you know; it's who you know," he often said. But in the back of my mind, I couldn't help but wonder—if he was so big and famous, why was he just an extra in a student film?

He claimed to have a talent agency and often talked about his good friends who were part of it. Eventually, he started sending me scripts, asking me to record auditions on my own and send them back to him.

Mistakes to Avoid: Part 2

It all felt a bit weird because they never felt like legit auditions and were never paid either. So, it all felt strange to me. I told him about Star Now too. He hadn't heard of it, which I thought was a bit odd.

I had the fear of needing to be loyal to him, and even though everything he was showing me was that he wasn't such a big superstar after all, I still had hope and a need to show my loyalty. If I backed off because I thought he was no good, that would not be being a loyal friend.

One day Simon came to a face-to-face audition with me, and afterwards, we met up with my friend Sarah. Simon ended up telling Sarah that he loved me.

That was too creepy for me. I backed off from him and I know he sensed it; he stopped calling me so much too.

After some time, he started posting pictures on Facebook of a new model he was getting modelling work for. It was a constant stream of posts. I suddenly felt a bit gutted, perhaps he was legit after all, and those were jobs I could have gotten? I also thought perhaps this new girl was his new love interest, and I would be safe from anything creepy. I liked his posts and commented once or twice.

Simon then called me, and we had our first phone call for the first time in a few months.

He didn't stop talking about the new model he had and was meeting up with. It sounded like I was safe from being his love interest.

F.G. Fraser

He posted on Facebook that he had two tickets to a film premiere and who would like to go with him? I commented saying that I would love to, thinking he wouldn't take me, but rather his new model friend.

I was so excited when he replied saying he would take me. I thought that perhaps he really was a good loyal friend, and his love was the genuine kind of love. I also had no idea that the film director of the film, Nigel, was friends with Simon on Facebook and reading the comments on his posts.

I can't remember if I added Nigel or Nigel added me, but I became Facebook friends with the film director. We then had an online video call with each other. He gave me a free ticket to his film premiere. He said it was mean of Simon to say I could go with him, but then take someone else.

I was so excited, and as the loyal friend I vowed to be, I let Simon know right away. I certainly didn't want to turn up alone and feel awkward wondering if I should approach Nigel and speak to him. I needed someone I knew to be safe to go with. I was also super keen to meet his new model friend, as I had seen many photos and had heard a lot about her.

We all had a very good evening and got a photo of us all together, Simon in his suit, and me and Samantha in our evening dresses. The photo of all three of us was the photo that got me my first featured speaking role in a big foreign movie. Simon was trying to get the role for Samantha, and the casting director pointed at me and was interested in me

Mistakes to Avoid: Part 2

instead. I love that story. It's almost similar to my dad's story as a child when he was naughty and ate his sister's share of the chocolate.

I always felt like I had to be even more loyal to Simon after that. If it wasn't for the photo he showed the casting director, I wouldn't have had my very first paid speaking role. It was super exciting, and I was terrified of looking like a fool. I managed to get it right on the second take. The first take was terrible. The casting director gave me more speaking roles after that. I was super grateful to him, too. I had a weird kind of love for him. He was making my dreams come true.

I still couldn't abandon Simon though. I wanted to make him proud. If I did well, then he would look good too, which I know is what he wanted.

I was friends with Simon for a long time. Looking back, they were extremely long years. It felt like a long time. I always felt good having a consistent friend for a long time.

During that time, he met other ladies who became a part of his agency.

After Samantha ditched him, he found a new model called Sammie. He used to talk about her a lot to me as well as another model called Harriet.

Harriet left his agency because he never got her any work, but kept posting posts of all the work she was getting for herself as if he were getting her the roles, which he wasn't.

Simon told me that after Sammie left him, she was a horrible person and just went around using people. He told me he hated her, and she wouldn't get away with it. He would bide his time, and she would get her comeuppance.

I met Sammie once and she told me that Simon loved me, like really loved me. I took that to be a friendship love, but now I am not so sure.

A couple of years later, Facebook posts kept popping up from other models and photographers I had met who all knew each other. "Sammie has gone missing, has anyone seen her? We have reported it to the police."

My blood ran cold as I read those posts. More than once, Simon had said to me, "She won't get away with it." Then, he called me a couple of times, insisting, "I would never hurt a woman; I would never do anything to her." Over the years, I've learned that when a man says this, he likely means the opposite. I pretended to believe him, but his other remarks kept replaying in my head. It's a frightening thought.

When I started meeting up with another friend, Larry, Simon began acting very weird. I think he must have gotten jealous. He became very creepy and was sending subliminal messages through Facebook. He posted a photo of one of his singing artists with her face all deranged. It looked like an acid attack. A couple of times over the years he would mention that an acid attack was one of the worst things you could do to another human being. Terror went through me and did for a long time after that.

Mistakes to Avoid: Part 2

I made it clear that I couldn't be friends with him anymore. I contacted a stalker charity and explained my situation. If you feel afraid of someone, then usually there is often a good reason for it.

Occasionally, I think of him, and I wonder what he is up to, but I know keeping away is the best option for both of us. I would only ever wish him well like I would wish anyone well.

What was my huge mistake here? Again, I wasn't trusting myself and I was giving my power away to someone else. We must always have total belief in ourselves and our journey. We will meet people along the way, but we shouldn't give away our power to them, in the hope for an easier ride.

I am sure Simon used to play all the other girls in his books against each other. I think he wanted us all to compete for his attention. One of the models, Nancy, whom he said was his "best friend" killed herself. It is probably just a total coincidence, but I also can't help thinking it is very strange.

I once saw her from a distance at an event and smiled at her, but I never spoke to her properly as I felt quite shy and like she was better than me. "She probably wouldn't want to talk to me," I thought. I do wish I had made a fearless effort with her though. Simon spoke about her often to me and told me many traumatic stories about her. My heart always went out to her with nothing but love.

When you come from an abused background, you can't help but allow other abusive people into your lives, until you finally break the cycle for good.

I think one of my reasons for becoming friends with Simon was; that I didn't feel I had many friends, and I didn't want to become a famous actress and not know who my real friends were. I realise now, to stay focused, and not let anyone distract you from that focus. There are so many snakes low down in the industry and it is easy to be sucked in if you have no self-worth or self-belief.

Simon believed in me, and it felt good. Besides my dad, I'd never had anyone believe in me and encourage me like that. Having someone from the industry who wasn't trying to have sex with me and who seemed genuinely interested in helping me progress was refreshing. Unfortunately, even men like that often have hidden agendas, even if it's just the desire to create a false relationship with you.

Chapter 13
Mistakes to Avoid: Part 3

With his persuasive chat, Simon sold my actress skills to the casting director, Lemar. While I was on set for my very first big movie, Lemar came over to me and said, "Where have you been hiding?"

After that, he would ask me if I was free for other roles. He would always give me a speaking role, and this was making my dreams come true. It felt incredibly good, and of course, I started to feel a bit of genuine love for him. I knew nothing could happen with him, and I never wanted it to, but I did feel a sort of love for him, for him trusting me with the roles and giving me the incredible experiences that he did. I felt so grateful, and even though I was paid for doing a job, I felt like I owed him something. I felt like I didn't deserve it. I think that is why my heart opened to him, so much with love.

Also, I guess, I was putting it on him and giving him the credit for it. Instead of continuing to believe in myself and my talent, and seeing that my talent was the reason he was giving me the roles. Even though I always knew it was just a professional relationship, he never gave me any sign it was anything else, or I didn't see it if he did. I couldn't help but have that love there. I suppose the love I felt, is the love I feel towards the whole of humanity, but it felt a little bit more special because I couldn't believe he was giving me all the acting roles. I loved it! I guess the fear Simon put into me about being loyal made me want to be loyal to Lemar too.

I did meet up with Lemar outside of work and we had a drink together. I did love him, but I still knew nothing more could happen. I guess I was happy we were friends, as I didn't have many friends apart from Simon, and Lemar felt good to be around, he never said anything threatening to me.

One day I met Lemar again because I had left my clothes at one of a film producer's locations and I needed to have them back. It was also nice that I was going to see Lemar again. I thought we would have a coffee, and maybe a bite to eat, and then I would head back home.

The next thing I knew he led me to a hotel, and we sat with his friend who was staying there in the lobby. I was a bit confused, and I felt uncomfortable. He poured us both a drink from a wine bottle and I suddenly felt like I was in danger. I'd had my drinks spiked in the past and was

Mistakes to Avoid: Part 3

paranoid that my drink had been spiked. I decided not to drink it, only having very tiny sips here and there to make it look like I was drinking.

He told me to drink it, so I just drank it and hoped for the best that I would be ok. I didn't want to be seen as being rude. I had no backbone or boundaries at this point.

He then led me upstairs to his friend's hotel room and I felt even more uncomfortable and confused.

I felt like this was not very professional either. He made us a cup of tea, and then he kept trying it on with me heavily. I kept refusing and pulling away from him. I was laughing nervously because I never understood it when men did this. I never believed that anyone could be truly malicious or think they were doing something wrong. I did have a bit of a love for him too. I had learned from my past that getting involved was not a good idea, and I was at a place where I felt strongly that I could set my boundary as a strong "no."

He kept pushing me, he got a little rough, but I pushed back. Because I liked him and was used to this behaviour from men; (you can read my first book, "Sex, Good or Bad," to read more of my stories and to learn more about men and get yourself into a loving relationship, if you struggle in that area). I refused to think he was doing anything wrong, and he got me speaking roles in movies. There was no way I was going to be "easy" and just sleep with him and give him what he wanted, however much I did like him. It wasn't professional, and he hadn't done enough to "woo" me or "court" me.

At one point, he asked me if I was scared; this tells me that perhaps he knew it was wrong. I was uncomfortable and I was a bit scared if I am honest. I wasn't attuned to my feelings, and I didn't think they were valid. This stems from the abuse I experienced as a child and the fact that I had found myself in this situation so many times before. What was there to be afraid of? I then used my acting skills on him, and in an aggressive seductive, "ok let's fuck" kind of voice I said, "You're the one who should be scared!"

He then stopped and looked at me for a while, perhaps he was trying to process what I had said.

He disappeared into the bathroom for what seemed to be about 20 minutes. I am not 100% sure what he was doing in there, but I think we can all guess.

After this interaction with Lemar, I felt disappointed. He had lost my trust, and I was confused. He never tried to meet up again after that, but I did another job for him, which I wasn't paid for. He wasn't there the day I did the job, and usually, we're given forms to fill out—which I had forgotten to do. Lemar had a reputation in the industry for not always paying actors, but I believed I was different. Perhaps not. Or maybe actors just forget about the form filling?

Mistakes to Avoid: Part 3

I learned once again that I needed to be stronger and more assertive. As soon as I saw him, I should have said, "I need to get back to the train station now. Thank you for giving me my dress back." (With low-budget films, you often have to provide your own costume.)

Chapter 14
Mistakes to Avoid: Part 4

When you get cast for a role, especially as a background artist, you meet other people who are doing the same as you. Often everyone adds each other on social media pages, and you realise that it is a community of many people who all know each other, and you eventually meet too. It is lovely and you start to feel like a bit of a family.

All these people you meet on set, many will have been doing it for a much longer time, and they know other casting directors who have been on social media and on all the relevant social media groups that put out castings.

One day in my Facebook messenger inbox a good friend messaged me and said he had had a casting for me; for a role in a movie that he had come across that he thought I could apply for.

Mistakes to Avoid: Part 4

I often had my ego up, thinking many roles were not good enough for me, but that was just a front, an excuse to cover up the anxiety I felt about going through the whole process. I did not apply for much, especially the type of movie it was for, as it was the same type of movie as the casting director, Lemar, whom I had met and gave me many roles. I also felt a sense of loyalty to him; I ought to not go elsewhere. That might have had something to do with Simon as well, though.

I was in a calm place and my ego wasn't present, so, I decided to just apply for it and see what happened. I received an email to say they would like to give me an audition.

I still wasn't overly excited, but I did want to do my best to do justice to the character as best I could. If I got it great and if I didn't, I knew that I had done my best and enjoyed the process.

It felt very good, and I was given the role. I was extremely happy and satisfied and almost couldn't believe it but decided to just enjoy it and go with the flow.

The day of the shoot arrived, and the other actress that had been cast, was very excited and upbeat all day. I just wanted to focus on getting my role right.

Whenever I had a background role, especially in the beginning, I used to act like her because I felt so excited to be on set and I couldn't believe I was there. Also, it might have had something to do with my buried ego wanting to be seen, "Look at me". There is nothing wrong with that as long as you're aware of it.

I ended up getting sucked into having lots of fun with her as we waited in the holding area. The holding area is where the actors and background artists are kept. Background artists and actors are usually kept in separate areas.

When I am acting, I usually stay focused and prepare to get into character, but this day I let her distract me. I liked the thought of connecting with another human being and making a friend. It also helped take my mind off what I was supposed to be doing which made me feel less anxious. It is easy to laugh around. When I am at work, I prefer to focus my mind and practice.

Once we got on set, she was very confident at miming with one of the main actors even though her back was to the camera. The camera was on me, and the director told me to mime with the main actor.

However, whenever the director called "action," the other actress continued to mime with the main actor. She was not listening to what the director wanted, and I didn't understand why she was bothering to mime when her back was to the camera.

Instead of me ignoring her and listening to the director, I let her miming distract me.

Mistakes to Avoid: Part 4

How could I convincingly pretend to have a conversation with the main actor when a 3rd person was doing all the talking? At the time I felt a bit upset and disappointed. Why was she continuing to mime? I wanted to be convincing, but talking over her wouldn't have been.

Looking back, I should have just ignored her and done what the director wanted. I wanted the director to instruct her not to speak so that I could do what he wanted. It didn't matter what she did; she had her back to the camera, which was facing me. I should have ignored her like she wasn't there. Damn it!

When I look back on this it makes me feel pissed off and annoyed. I was unable to make the director think, "Yes, I am so glad I chose her!" The actress was not listening to the director and kept chatting as if she was being seen.

That was a huge mistake that I regret. I should have told her not to mime as it puts me off doing what I have been told.

Not just with actors but in my main life I need to be more assertive and say what I want to happen. The director clearly said what he wanted, and I should have used my blocking acting skills. I should have done it like she wasn't there. I should have done my bit talking over her as if she wasn't even in the conversation we were having.

Another mistake I made was getting too friendly with other actresses and actors, most of whom I would probably never see again. The key to seeing directors again and working with them is by making the director happy. This is the most important part of acting. It's incredibly satisfying when I nail it, and the looks of love and gratitude I receive are just fantastic—truly fulfilling.

Chapter 15
Mistakes to Avoid: Part 5

One day scrolling through the list of auditions on Star Now, I came across an audition for a TV series paying £300 a day. The thought of me landing a role in it got me excited and I applied for it, hoping I might at least get an audition.

I did get an audition! I was sent a list of characters with an outline for each character and a back story, and I was told to make something up for the audition.

It made me feel a bit sick, as I hate not having a script to work with. I decided I would do it anyway and come up with something, anything at all. I never had to see them again!

I did my piece at the audition, and I felt so nervous. The lady auditioning gave me some advice and I did my piece again taking her advice.

I wasn't sure if I would get it or not after that. I didn't think being taught at an audition was a good thing, even though I thoroughly enjoyed the buzz of it all.

I couldn't believe it when I received an email telling me I had gotten the role. I was ecstatic and over the moon. I never told anyone though, not even my family because I wanted it to become real and let them see it for themselves. I used to be like that with all my roles, and I am kind of still like it now. Partly because often, we are made to sign a form agreeing to rules and some of those rules are to not mention to anyone that you're doing it, not the name of production or anything.

I guess deep down I didn't believe it could be real. An online casting website that anyone can join? A TV series that paid £300 a day?

After I was told I had gotten the role, I was then told I needed to put together a monologue for the character I had been given. I was told that before we started filming, a stage show would be put on, and I would perform the monologue on a stage in front of an audience.

It felt extremely unsettling, and it was not like I was close to achieving my dreams at all. I was embarrassed to invite anyone close to me, like close family and friends, but I did want some people to come. I wanted it to be real, and I wanted the show to be real. I invited some friends that I had met along the way who were also in the industry; like those I met on the set of a movie, or at an event, or somewhere

Mistakes to Avoid: Part 5

else, but they were all people who were into acting, dancing, music, or modelling.

I had 2 rehearsals for the stage show. This too was a huge red flag as I had to rehearse over the phone. It felt extremely weird!

The first one I was just at home and saying the lines. I didn't perform at all. I just said the lines to ask if the script was ok.

Luckily, the 2nd time I stayed with a friend in the army at the barracks in London. I then felt even more embarrassed because I had told him about the rehearsal I was doing over the phone, so I had to make it much better especially if there was the potential that he might see or listen.

I just went for it. A full-force performance, on my own in his room and on the telephone. Bizarre!

BUT . . . I DID IT, and the guy on the phone said it sounded much better than the first time. Duh!! I didn't perform the first time around!!

It was good that I had an audience to feel uncomfortable around. What did the army soldier know about rehearsals? Perhaps they're sometimes done over the phone?

Anyway, I was mortified at the thought of getting up on a stage and performing. I had done some plays and musicals at school and thoroughly loved being given lines to learn. I even had speech and drama lessons and got a Distinction for a LAMDA exam, which I always felt proud of. But, when I was a teenager, I felt very awkward going to theatre school and I had the belief that I was not able to be an actress performing on a stage.

Even though I was pretty sure that the TV series wasn't going to come to fruition, I still couldn't bring myself to pull out. Just in case!! What did I have to lose? A bit of travel money to get to the location?

A good friend of mine that I was meeting up with quite a lot at that time was Richard, another award-winning film director. I think something in me thought that if I was able to meet up with an award-winning film director and a TV director who had directed many well-known TV shows as well as two famous soaps, Emmerdale Farm and Brookside; if I could be friends with someone that did this, then I too could be on a TV series.

I invited Richard to the show, and I invited some others to come along to the show - they all had to buy tickets for this stage show. Even more obvious that the £300 a day acting role wasn't real. I did feel silly and humiliated, but I was desperate for it to be real. I was also going through the "twin flame hell" chapter of my first book, "Sex: Good or Bad?" That was similar. Wanting a relationship to be real that wasn't and experiencing a near-death experience because of it.

I was desperate to make it look real though. I even paid for a couple of friends' tickets, to make sure they came.

Mistakes to Avoid: Part 5

"I had an audition for a TV series, got the role, and was now going to be performing on a stage". This is what I told everyone, which is exactly what I was told, and was super keen to believe it.

I did it and it felt crazy to do it. I was super shy, and acting on stage in front of an audience when I believed I had no training for it was terrifying. Especially as underneath I thought this was going to be a £300 a day TV series role, which I kind of also knew it wasn't.

I didn't have it in me to let the production down. It felt easier to let them take me for a ride and make me look like a fool. Perhaps that is what made me go with the blatant red flags that told me it wasn't real. I felt bad pulling out; and to go through with it, I had to believe it was real! That probably sounds more like it!

When I met up with Richard after the stage show, he told me if the finance for the TV series hasn't even been approved and the pilot and first episode haven't even been written, then the team of people putting it together, don't have a say who the actors and actresses will be.

My mistake here was not looking at the red flags . . . HOWEVER . . .

F.G. Fraser

Every Cloud has a Silver Lining

All mistakes we make in life are lessons and experiences and now I can share mine with you in this book, just to make sure you too don't make the same mistakes as me.

The fake TV series I auditioned for was an amazing experience for me. The fact that I did it, that I got up on stage and performed. I got the role and if I was so awful they wouldn't have chosen me. Any chance to practice our acting craft is amazing. This was a chance for me to practice.

I probably should have gotten myself into acting classes and done more acting at a film school. That is another reason I was adamant about believing it was real so that I could practice my craft, which is what all of us actors should be doing all of the time.

I recently signed up for Amy Jo Berman's acting coaching and also purchased some of her courses, which I am looking forward to getting stuck into. I am sure I could write a much better and more informative book after taking her courses. I have been receiving her emails for years but have been unable to afford them. I am super excited to get stuck in.

She has already given me an amazing piece of advice which is, "Yes, sure that would be great." Ask them for their social media sites and follow them, stay on their radar!"

Mistakes to Avoid: Part 5

She told me this after I told her about not getting auditions, but then casting directors were asking me if I would be interested in working with them in the future. This was a mistake, being too shy to be upfront and staying on these filmmakers' radars. Being big, bold, confident, strong, and knowing that I am amazing and most definitely good enough for whatever role comes my way!

Chapter 16
Dissipate the ego

This chapter may be difficult to read as it exposes the ego, and the ego doesn't like to be exposed. Do try and get through it until the end though.

Notice that the chapter heading is titled "Dissipate THE Ego" and not "Dissipate YOUR ego". It is not your ego; it is a separate part of you that every single one of us has. The ego is something that we can be aware of.

If this chapter does get difficult, keep in mind that eradicating the ego is an important part of acting. You need to be completely authentic and raw at your core, and then you can start developing the layers of the character on top of your core. This chapter will help in being able to do that by exposing the ego so you can work on being present and know what it is like to be the real you, without all the parts of you that have just been created since you were born.

Dissipate the ego

The ego is the part of us that thinks it is separate from others.

Examples of ego thinking include, "I am better than them," "I want to be the best," "I am a victim, in pain, and no one understands," or "Those people understand, let's group together," or in Eckhart Tolle's simple words, the ego is an identity. Eckhart is aware that his identity is now that of a "spiritual teacher."

The ego creates suffering. When it has been deflated, it hurts. In extreme cases it enjoys creating suffering in others because of the personal pain it believes it has suffered. If we were able to surrender the ego totally, no one would ever feel any suffering at all. This is why when I completely nail an acting role it feels like magic. Anything heavy weighing me down is lifted and I feel light and free. Watching myself back on the screen is fascinating because I look like I am not acting at all. It is incredible. I am just being.

The ego is revengeful and likes to get revenge. "You hurt me, so I will hurt you!" Some egos believe that others are out to cause them pain and are extremely guarded. The ego can also feel threatened in someone else's presence, and for no reason, it creates drama and negativity.

When we are aware of our egos, we can start to practice letting go of the negativity that the ego enjoys feeling and we can watch the reaction or action it wants us to do. By being aware and feeling through it, knowing that it is not our true self, we can practice letting go and not following through with the ego's demands and wanting to be right.

The Ego Wants

The ego seeks love and the feeling of being loved, often equating power with being loved. It fails to recognize that your true self is pure essence—already embodying love and immense power. Power can be gentle. In acting for the camera, less is more. The camera captures every tiny movement. Because of the ego's lack of awareness, it is the cause of anything that doesn't feel good, and the ego believes it can make itself feel good by doing (revenge for example) or having something external from your inner self or arguing a point to make itself right.

When we see successful actors and actresses getting lots of attention from the media, it can make us want the same, that is our ego. The ego seeks admiration from others. This can cause the ego to suffer when it desires something, such as an acting role, during an audition. If you go to an audition desperate to get the role, you will most likely not get it; however, if you go wanting to nail the role, regardless of the outcome, you are much more likely to be able to lose your ego and get the role, or at least not be disappointed that you did not get the role and happy that you did your best.

Whenever the ego feels its power being taken away, it reacts. The ego can get in the way if you feel too disappointed.

Dissipate the ego

You may stop applying for acting roles, or the disappointment will just carry through to the rest of your life. You must view auditions as part of the fun.

Some people know their true selves and have had glimpses of their pure essence. They have felt the love that they are and have connected to their true selves, but then their ego takes over, and instead of feeling it and being connected to it, they believe they know it all, and this is the ego. The ego fights to survive, and instead of seeing it as something bad, which is also the ego, we must use it for positive effects. If we see it as bad, we can be taken advantage of by other bigger and more bad egos.

Another thing the ego does a lot of is to judge. You will find yourself judging your self-tapes, and judging your performance, but the worst thing it judges is other actors you meet along the way and become social media buddies with. Never let your ego compare yourself to their headshots or what they are up to. Their acting journey is completely different to yours and we can only focus on our own journey.

When we allow the ego to judge others, we don't see their perfect inner essence and when we judge our performances, it is taking us away from our perfect inner essence and the part connected to God that creates miracles and gives us the roles we want. We come out of flow, and life is more difficult.

F.G. Fraser

Hello Good Looking

Nature has it so that people are attracted to physical good looks. This is the healthy gene pool, and everyone wants to procreate with healthy genes.

It is the ego that desperately wants a person with physical attractiveness. It is the ego that wants a good-looking person.

Actors and actresses in Hollywood are mostly incredibly physically attractive. People like looking at attractive people so this would be the reason why. You may get some unattractive actors and actresses or plain-looking ones; I won't name any as this is also the judging ego. Deep down at everyone's core, we're all perfectly beautiful and exactly how God created us to be.

If you're an incredibly good-looking person and think that is enough to get you all the acting roles you want, you are mistaken. That is the ego. (I am hoping to prepare you for disappointment, so your ego won't react negatively.) Breathe into it and be aware of any negative reactions. Awareness is key to help dissipate the ego.

It can help if you have good industry standard headshots, and you have the right colouring the casting director is looking for, but you also need to create the character the casting director wants to see. Sometimes a casting director is only looking for a specific look, this is the one we are all hoping for.

Dissipate the ego

When a man or woman with a big ego about their appearance, thinks that they are successful in acting because of it, they will stop trying and think that acting roles easily come to them for that reason and will end up being hugely disappointed with future outcomes.

Having talent in acting, is always the main reason for success. It is not the ego if you think you are talented, and it is the truth. If you have experienced getting acting roles after auditions, then this is evidence of the talent you have. The ego can disguise itself in many ways. The ego can always find a way to make you suffer.

The ego wants to be powerful and the main way we are seen as powerful on planet Earth is with money. So, fortune as well as fame is something the ego aspires to possess. Wanting to get to the top in acting, i.e. Hollywood, can get us millions of pounds per film. It is the ego that wants to get to the top for this reason.

We must let go of wanting that. We must just enjoy the process of getting there. Eradicating the ego, staying present, and enjoying the journey is how to do it. The ego will just hold you back.

My survival brain allowed my ego to hold me back because it felt safe. It was familiar and not risky. Staying on benefits was my survival method, and working too much would take that away from me. My faith in God and my journey wasn't strong enough to let that go. That was from God, and

I appreciated it. I had forgotten that God is abundant and will always give me more and keep on giving and giving.

Ego and Feelings

The ego doesn't like uncomfortable feelings, and will often react negatively and blame someone else for it, or instead, will push them away and cover it up, pretending they're not there.

The following paragraph shows you an amazing practice for eradicating the ego.

Keeping as aware as you can in each moment of how you feel, every time an uncomfortable feeling comes up, welcome it with awareness. Let it override you and allow yourself to feel the discomfort and notice that you are just the watcher of it, and you will then feel a sense of calm and peace after it has disappeared.

The ego is also the part of us that feels uncomfortable, negative, and victimised around people that it sees as more powerful than it. It is also the part of us that feels excited and overwhelmed with positive feelings, placing the positive feelings onto the other person when this is always our true state of being with ourselves.

If you see someone else as having an ego or being more powerful than you, this too is your ego. "What we see in others is a reflection of ourselves."

Dissipate the ego

Understanding this statement, "What we see in others is a reflection of ourselves," also helps us to eradicate our ego and become a whole human being, just with ourselves. If we can stay aware of our thoughts about others, we can then look at our egos more closely, allowing ourselves to feel uncomfortable with them, dissipating another layer of them, and allowing us to see the truth.

When we can stay connected to our true selves, the purest form of love deep within, we can then stay calm and respond to negative or positive situations in an authentic way.

Powerful people, like all people, react positively when you are authentically yourself and not feeling attached to or dependent on others—this is attractive. Imagine being on set with a Hollywood actor, and they come over to chat, hold your hand, or stand as close to you as possible. (OMG! When this happened, my ego reacted immediately. My inner thoughts were, "How dare you think you can stand that close to me!" Did I move? Nope, that was my ego too: "I am not moving!" But the truth was, I LOVED how close this Hollywood heartthrob stood next to me, lol!)

When I got an acting role after an audition, I had the ego hold me back, but the shame of disappointing the film director forced me to feel it fully, then go overly wild and shake it off, refusing to feel embarrassed (remember how painfully shy I can be in some situations?) and then diminish the ego and feel the magic of performing perfectly. It does feel like magic, yet rewatching the film footage is incredible, because it looks so normal, like a real person. Effortless! WOW!

One of the warm-up exercises I learned at film school is to go overly wild, it does feel good forcing yourself to not give a f*** what others think of you. It can be in that moment performing, but also outside when you're thinking what family and friends think, do I look good? This is the ego!! Do it because you love the magic of it!

Me, Me, Me Ego!

Even when they're not performing, actors and actresses are frequently viewed as being extremely dramatic. Some of them may be doing it to appease their egos, but most of the time they are just expressing themselves, and anyone who finds fault with that is making an assumption based on their ego.

Some actors and actresses most probably are "me, me, and me" This is good for theatre acting and being seen by the audience at the back, but with film and TV, it is not good to be like this.

I have worked as a background artist many times and I see this with other background artists. It is quite comical because they are in the background, yet they do their best to position themselves in front of the camera and for as long as possible. The camera picks up on this easily and it could destroy the scene.

Dissipate the ego

When being an actor and your full face is on camera, you can never look into the camera, and you can never let the audience know that you know the camera is there. You must be completely shut off and oblivious to it after the director shouts "action". I am very sensitive when watching film and TV; I can always tell when an actor is aware of the camera and not fully immersed in his or her role.

My painful shyness came in handy for me for this, for me to perform I had to shut off the camera. It was almost a survival mechanism for me. I am so used to doing it now, that I am no longer afraid; I just really enjoy immersing myself in the character and feeling the magic that comes with it.

A background artist must also do the same. I remember on set not thinking I would ever be shown as I am never usually in the background, but I remember the camera pointing right at me and me thinking, "It is not looking at me, and even if it is, I am not reacting to it." I just enjoyed staying in my role even though I believed I would not be shown. The main actor even came over to me on this day and asked me how my dinner was, in his character. It was such an incredible moment.

When I went to watch the movie, there was a clear shot of me standing up and clapping. It was very exciting to see. Completely ignoring the camera is how you get shown, because let's be honest, that is what we would love to see, that is the most fun part.

It is exciting, and we must allow ourselves to be happy and excited with calm awareness. I used to numb myself from it, and tell myself "It's not that good, you can do better!"

"I am a victim" ego

The "I am a victim" ego identity is used to being treated badly, and is comfortable with familiarity, so it pulls you back from becoming great. It will blame others from your past for treating you badly and in acting it will blame others for not believing in you and telling you, 'You can't do it.'

You know deep down you can do whatever you want to. Focus on the words of positivity and not the words of negativity. It is the ego that likes to dwell on the negative, to keep you in victim mode.

Thoughts

Thoughts are what can create suffering. Thoughts are just the ego. Thoughts that another is more amazing than us and more influential; make you feel smaller than your equally powerful loving self. Thoughts that we're not good enough and thoughts of the past and what we want to do in the future, all thoughts take you out of the present moment and into your head.

Dissipate the ego

When you're performing, you have to just be. No thinking about the next line of dialogue, the words must flow out of your mouth as if it is the very first time you have said it while BEING the character. A lot of actors act and are doing acting, but amazing acting is being.

Of course, you have to learn your lines; you will be saying them over and over again out loud and like me, in your head while out and about on walks and in public. Embarrassingly, if you're like me, sometimes the feeling or emotion will be expressed on your face at the same time. That can be embarrassing to the ego when it is realised.

Who cares? You know you're rehearsing, so just let it be, feel the discomfort, dissipate it, and continue.

You must have faith and confidence in yourself that you know the lines, then when it comes to performing, you can just let go and be.

Often, with my best performances, I close my eyes and imagine watching myself exactly how I would do it, going in deep, going through the lines calmly, getting in the zone, then "action" and just being. I have gone really deep, so deep down, kind of the stomach, but far away from the head. Blackness deep.

Thinking about your lines, or the next line you have, is not staying in the present moment, and wondering how the last line went is also not being fully present and BEING. When you master it and nail it, it feels truly like magic.

F.G. Fraser

Unfortunately, I don't have time to edit and add to this book the "feelings" chapter from my first book, titled, "Sex Good or bad?"

However, when I was doing the 4 weeks "acting for film" course recently, I realised that the practices and tools I suggest in that chapter, could help actors on their acting journey.

Email me at fgfraserbooks@gmail.com with the subject being, "FEELINGS chapter ORDER" and I will send you the digital version of the "Feelings" chapter from my first book for free, no charge.

Alternatively, I can send you the complete book in the paperback version for less than half price, £9.69 + postage and packaging. Email me at fgfraserbooks@gmail.com with the subject being, "BOOK ORDER Sex: Good or Bad?"

*This price is at the time of printing 2025

Thank You

Thank you, Alfie, my amazing, gorgeous son, I am so lucky to always have your love. I love you so much, and could not have continued through life without you, to achieve my dreams.

Thank you, Adnan, my lovely husband and supporter for all I do. Thank you for everything you do and for always listening and being understanding and patient.

Thank you to my amazing dad, my late father, he always believed in me and always supported me on my acting journey, and was the first to implant the idea that I could become a film and TV actress. Miss you so much but I know the power you introduced me to is still guiding me, and showing me the way.

Thank you, Beth Kingston-Jones, the actress who played India in Hollyoaks and who directed me onto the right path in my acting journey.

F.G. Fraser

Thank you to Anis Yahyaoui for encouraging me to go for my first-ever real film shoot, for which I was successful in the casting I applied for. Thank you, Thank you, Thank you!

Thank you so much to the late Philip Chan, for always encouraging me and helping me on my journey, even landing me an incredible acting role! Miss you so much, but your memory helps me carry on. Thank you!

Thank you, Scott Hilliar for all your advice, and support, and thank you for recommending your agent to me. She was awesome and lovely just like you said she would be.

Thank you, Tracey Hall, for taking me onto your books and allowing me to audition for the incredible roles you put me forward for. I loved all our interactions and I hope you enjoy reading my book.

Thank you, Manoj Anand for all the castings you have sent me and continue to do so. I appreciate you a lot. Thank you.

Thank you, A. P. Wilding, for all the fantastic headshots and other shots you have taken of me.

Thank you, Amy Jo Berman, for all the acting coaching you have given me so far and all the acting coaching to come. I am super excited to have you on my journey.

Thank you, Daniel Eghan for recommending Talent Talks agency to me and for all the fun times we have had on set together.

Thank You

Thank you to the Talent Talks team, Gemma Gurvitz, Steve Robbins, Bobby Mitchell, and everyone else, thank you for sending me auditions and all the extremely fun roles I landed through your agency over the years. Also, for the incredibly fun summer party you hold each year.

Thank you to the actor Tal Profs for your advice that I have included in the castings/auditions chapter.

Thank you to the people I write about in the "mistakes to avoid" chapters, you helped me progress amazingly and gave me some incredible experiences on my journey. For that, I will always have a place in my heart for you. (Not the dodgy film director though! He is non-existent to me now, thank God!)

Thank you, Sarah Warren, for being my first ever acting tutor at MET film school. I have never forgotten that incredible weekend!

Thank you, Arkie Reece, my incredibly amazing acting tutor at MET film school.

Thank you to all the other knowledgeable tutors who taught us along the way in our 4-week acting for film course, Giles, Trevor Murphy, Gordon, Janis Jaffa and Neil West.

Extra special thanks to Giles, the voice coach, I can't thank him enough for what he taught me to do with my voice. I just to practice consistently every day! Thank you! I have serious love for God/Allah for placing Giles on my path, love him!

Thank you, Jack Ryder, for all your amazing coaching sessions. I am looking forward to many more to come and achieving even more success.

Thank you, Mum, for being my lovely mum and babysitting Alfie when you did so I could experience my lifelong dreams.

Thank you, Emily Fraser, my lovely older sister, you confirmed my longing to be an actress to be true when that used to be your dream when we were kids. I always thought you were amazing and wanted to be just like you. All though, I never changed my dream when you changed yours.

Thank you Clemi Fraser for also sharing in the acting dream and being my amazing younger sister!

Thank you, Sonia Ashworth, for being my lovely Godmother and being one of the loveliest people I have ever known on planet Earth, and for letting me sleep over when I had a film job close by to you.

Thank you so much Katie Broad for being one of my greatest ever friends and giving me the longest real true connection with another beautiful being in this crazy world. I love you more than you could know.

Thank you, thank you, thank you so much to Sallie, Keith, and Paige Mabry for always helping me out when I asked you to babysit Alfie for me so I could go off and be on the set of films. Honestly WOW! THANK YOU!!

Thank You

Thank you, Deborah Jay Kelly, for seeing the good in me and showing me lots of care on my journey. You have helped increase my confidence tremendously, and I have met so many wonderful people along the way. I love you dearly and I am so grateful and relieved to have you in my life. Can't wait to see you. Miss you!

Thank you, Richard Standeven, for being a cool friend and writing the foreword for both of the books I have written.

Thank you, Carlos M Fandango, for giving me a wonderful testimonial, following my advice, and achieving your own results.

Thank you, Thierry Porter, for being an incredible human on my journey and making lots of fun with me on the 2 days we were on set together.

Thank you, Lukas Di Sparrow, for being a fun friend to hang out with, and thank you for teaching me how to use the "You Cut" video editor and for the awesome acting sessions you put together for everyone when we first met.

Thank you, Stuart Waite, for your generosity, and kindness throughout the years.

Thank you, Jamie Johnson for introducing me to boxing and the gym I enjoy going to now, and also for inviting me to Vegas when you won your award. You're awesome! Big love!

F.G. Fraser

Thank you, Dorothy Koomson, best-selling author for being such an amazing inspiration to me to write my books. Loads of love!

Thank you to Vishal, and my book angel Kim for being so supportive and encouraging on my book writing journey. Book number 2 is here, WOW!

Thank you, Ben Allsop, at Shape Your Destiny, for always showing me true love, and kindness, for all your patience, and for never giving up on wanting to coach me.

Thank you to everyone else in the Shape Your Destiny coaching group for always being a great support.

Extra special thanks to Naomi Sandler for putting me up, but also for putting up with me for 4 weeks when I did the acting for film course. I hope to stay again when I land more acting roles. You're the loveliest most calm and gentle person I have ever met, and your air B&B is not only extremely comfortable but also in a super convenient location!

Thank you, Christine Flynn, mine, and Alfie's Nan for always being there and continuing to love me after reading my first book. Alfie and I will miss you always. Rest peacefully and we will forever enjoy the memories you made with us, and the love in our hearts will be eternal. 9th February 1947 – 21st January 2024.

Thank You

Lastly, and most incredibly, thank you so much to the highest almighty power, Allah/God, for saving me every time I call out, for always answering my prayers, and for all the amazing, wonderful souls disguised as people that you so generously placed on my journey called life. Thank you! I know there are many more incredible encounters to come. THANK YOU! THANK YOU! THANK YOU!

Other Book Titles by the author F G Fraser

Sex: Good or Bad? – End the cycle of toxic encounters and create a loving and fulfilling relationship.

Don't be fooled by the title of F.G. Fraser's first book—it's not just about sex. This book is eye-opening and contains a deeply spiritual element. F.G. Fraser shares some deeply personal stories, including her own cheeky experience in Amsterdam, 2 separate horrifying experiences where she was almost murdered by men who said they loved her or wanted to marry her. Then there is also a story from an anonymous lady, Jessica, whose name changed to protect her identity, of her incredible, blissful, but shocking orgasmic experience on a one-night stand.

This book will take you on an incredible journey, which, according to many readers who have expressed to F G Fraser, made them cry.

Exciting book titles coming soon . . .

Diets/Fasting: Good or Bad? – Why do I have a Gastric sleeve and is it something you should consider?

F G Fraser shares her experience with a lifetime of struggles with food and exercise. With social media glamourizing going abroad for cheap surgeries she wants to share her truth which shines light on the dark side of it all.

If you have ever thought about having a gastric sleeve or are desperate to lose weight and feel like you have tried everything, Francesca can share some incredible tips and information with you, to help you make the best decision for yourself.

Autism at mainstream school: Good or Bad?

The author shares her struggles at school and in life, including the panic she felt when her son received a diagnosis and the challenges he faced. When her son left school and failed to get into college, she was finally directed to the proper support and help for him. She outlines the steps you need to apply for extra special needs support so your child can thrive and not be overlooked, as she and her son once were.

Charity Boxing: Good or Bad? - Can violence ever be justified?

F G Fraser shares her experience of when she was guided by various signs to enter a charity boxing match. She shares stories about her past that got her involved in physical fights in her adolescent years which led her to feel guilt for many years. She also shares the abuse and bullying she experienced as a child that she believes gave her the mindset to be able to enter the boxing match. She believes the signs that guided her were from God so she can share her knowledge in this book with you.

If you would like to order or pre-order any of my books at a discounted price, please send me an email to fgfraserbooks@gmail.com with the subject in CAPITAL letters "BOOK ORDER!" and the title.

For example, "BOOK ORDER! Sex Good or Bad?"

If you would like a signed copy, please request it in the email. I look forward to all your emails.

Printed in Dunstable, United Kingdom